THE

KIND
SELF-HEALING

BOOK

D1529847

This book is designed to assist with self-healing based on practices that have worked for the author. The exercises are intended as a supplement to personal growth work and therapy, but not as a replacement for it.

Published by:
Last House Press
885 Olive Street
Petaluma, CA 94952

ISBN: 978-0-9863063-0-3

For individuals or groups interested in a workshop or workshop series based on the materials in this workbook, contact the author at amyeden@guesswhatnormalis.com.

Written requests for reuse of this book's content should be sent to amyeden@guesswhatnormalis.com.

Illustrations by Marla Pedersen of www.ripplestudio.net
Book design by Stacey Aaronson

Printed in the United States of America

THE
KIND
SELF-HEALING
BOOK

RAISE YOURSELF UP

WITH

CURIOSITY AND COMPASSION

AMY EDEN

LAST HOUSE PRESS

CONTENTS

PART FOUR: CARING FOR YOU

Acknowledgments

Without the readers of my blog, Guess What Normal Is, this book wouldn't exist. Thank you for reading the blog, sharing your stories and struggles, reaching out by email, and your virtual high-fives. Without the encouragement of wise therapist Jay Talkoff, there would be no workbook, just daydreams. I wouldn't have chosen this life journey, but I am, at last, thankful that it is mine.

Crossing paths with artist Marla Pedersen was an act of Miss Fortuna spinning her great wheel and bestowing magic upon this project. Thank you, Marla. Your talent is breathtaking, and your work elevated this book.

While I wrote the book, Stacey Aaronson is responsible for making this book. She designed the gorgeous interior and incredible cover. She took my raw manuscript and seemed to magically create a book from it. I'm grateful to Stacey and admire her publishing wisdom, respect for detail, and sympathetic guidance every step of the way.

Sara Bixler, Annika Nelson Erickson, Claire Jeffers, Tim Jollymore, Megan Malone, Wendy Ostroff, Chad St. Clair, Kim Ribeiro, Carol Squicci, and Erin Wrightsman kindly gave the manuscript their scrutiny and care, finding typos in the final hours before the book went into production (despite the fact that I forgot to retrieve their scones from the oven!). Thank you.

Karen Beard, thank you for scanning the many, many hand-drawn illustrations for this book and your enthusiasm for what you saw!

Four extraordinarily generous individuals—and extraordinarily generous is not an exaggeration—Michael Giotis, Susan Koechner, Heather Henry Rawlins, and Ryan Willard read the book from start to finish and provided feedback integral to the book's becoming balanced, clear, powerful, and accurate. Mike challenged my ideas, Susan spotted even the most invisible of typos, Heather chuckled along with me in spirit and raised my message to a higher bar, and Ryan dusted off my language to let the courage shine through. Thank you.

The publishing of this book was made possible by an important group of individual kind souls and true believers. Never before have I felt like others had my back—now I do. This book was crowd-source funded through IndieGoGo.com (bit.ly/kindbook). In all, 143 individuals donated to the project, making it possible for you to hold this book in your hands. I am indebted to them. The following folks gave extra support, in alphabetical order:

Rose Anderson

Diane Aronld-Stamper

Halldóra Ásmundsdóttir

Marín Ásmundsdóttir

Smári Ásmundsson

Jennifer Aument

Karen Beard

Anna Chiara Bellini

Jen Birmingham

Sara Bixler

Veronica Blaustein

Vincent Casaliana

Erica Claggett

Marylene Cloitre

Michael Davis

Alex DeMambro

Kaisa and Ky Dille Dickens

Deborah Leigh Dille

Erin Eisenhaur

Annika Nelson Erickson

Katayoun Fazio

Caleb Ferguson

Adam Flaherty

Jordan Duane Frantz

Rachel Galdamez

Marcelo Gioria

Johnny Gray

Janell Hampton

Marsee Henon

Jessica Hopeman

Maureen Jennings

Nicholas Jollymore

Tim Jollymore

Andrew Kay

Susan Koechner

Mary Lundberg

Aerlia McLaird

Meredith Madden

Megan and Ian Malone

Ashish Mogera

Jessicca Moore

Debbie Moran

Patrick and Lexi Murray

Molly Newman

Jon Peddie

Marla Pedersen

Matt Pepe

Philippe Perebinossoff

Sara Peyton

Silke Puppich

Heather Henry Rawlins

Kim Ribeiro

Simon St. Laurent

Amy Selverston

Carol Squicci

Daniel Stauffer

Lisa Wagenbach

Erin Wrightsman

Jay Youngdahl

This book is dedicated to the readers of my blog,
guesswhatnormalis.com

And the day came for the risk
it took to remain tight
inside the bud was more
painful than the risk it took
to blossom.

—ANAÏS NIN

PREFACE

When you've had a less than perfect childhood, there is healing work to be done. When you've experienced a great trauma in your life, there is healing work to be done. When you're a person living in this world, there's healing work to be done—to be human is to experience pain, and to be human is to be, by nature, a transformation-prone being.

✦ ✦ ✦ ✦ ✦ ✦

Perhaps you wonder if this is the right book for you. If your childhood didn't quite prepare you for adulthood, your answer to most of the questions on the next two pages will be "yes." If your childhood home wasn't the place to just be yourself and perfection was expected of you, it's high time you bravely embrace the real, imperfect you. If your family's code was pretending things were fine when they weren't, you're in the right place. If you were expected to be glad when you were sad, you're not alone. If you've come into adulthood battling low self-worth and the nagging sense that you're different from other people, you're reading the right book.

Regardless of how much these questions resonate with you the first time you read through them, know this: anyone is welcome on this journey.

✶ Do you have trouble saying "no"?

✶ Do you overcommit yourself, say "yes," then panic?

✶ Do you seek approval from others only to need more?

✶ Are you self-critical?

✶ Is perfection your ultimate goal?

✶ Do you need to feel that you're "in control"?

✶ Would you rather control others than trust them?

✶ Are you doubtful about the outcome of acting on your instincts?

✶ Do you feel shame about who you really are?

✶ Do you have trouble completing projects and tasks?

✶ Do you struggle to get places on time? (Are you always 5–15 minutes late?)

✶ Do you "go numb," feel fuzzy-headed, or feel like your brain locks down during a conflict?

✶ Do you feel your life is one big, unfurling reaction to what happened to you in childhood?

✶ Are you always waiting for the bottom to drop out?

✶ Do you feel your life is driven by things people did, and still do, to you?

✶ Do you fear that if you finally reveal the true you that you'll be rejected?

✶ Is it difficult, or even scary, for you to ask for what you want?

✶ Do intimate relationships scare you?

✶ Are you unsure whether you have a right to get mad—really mad?

✶ Do you question whether you have a right to your feelings?

✶ Do you experience anxiety that leads to panic attacks?

✶ Do you imagine future conversations, plot, or plan ahead and then get upset by the actual result, which differs from your expectations?

* Do you believe your feelings are connected to, dependent on, or control the emotions of other people?

* Do you feel more comfortable around chaos or people with big problems?

* Are you afraid that if you change, you'll be rejected by your family or that you'll be rejecting them?

* Do you find yourself wondering why you didn't say "no" earlier, stand up for yourself, or get out of a scenario much sooner?

* Is being self-reflective, idle, or "lazy" uncomfortable for you?

* Is it difficult for you to just let go and have fun?

* Do you crave, yet fear, spontaneity?

Five Super-Kind Abilities You'll Gain from Doing This Work

Each of these abilities is within your reach. They develop from practice and applying a compassionate approach to your personal growth—and from a decision to take the leading role in your own story every day.

1. You'll become self-propelled.

The fuel driving your actions will become *your* wants, desires, and needs rather than your fear and anxiety about other peoples' needs or wants. Your own unique interests, goals, and personal fulfillment will become more central in guiding how you participate in life.

2. You'll become able to handle highly charged situations.

The discomfort you feel when asking for what you want and during confrontations will become a manageable one—a low simmer rather than a high flame—and you'll regard and appreciate the increasing comfort you have while dealing with difficult conversations as encouraging proof of having become daring and engaged in life.

3. Your self-esteem will become sturdy.

Your self-esteem will become more consistent and less of a roller-coaster ride, and you'll experience more and longer-lasting hopeful moments of ease and self-appreciation because you'll have cultivated unconditional love for yourself and ceased to expect perfection of your every breath.

4. You'll learn to stay calm when criticized.

You'll be able to remain calm in situations involving criticism without losing your sense of self, your core, and your self-esteem; you'll be able to hear and benefit from criticism without the old and unhelpful party-crashers of anger, fear, and defensiveness.

5. You'll learn to comfortably express your needs.

You'll become comfortable expressing yourself and your needs in romantic relationships and willing to risk an ending rather than stay in a problematic situation; you will never again rationalize disrespect, criticism, or manipulation just to keep a situation going. And you won't be tempted to try controlling the relationship because you'll have moved from living in your head to living in the present moment.

THE LIES THAT BIND: DYSFUNCTIONAL FAMILIES

If there is a problem in a family and its members don't want to fix it, the family will become dysfunctional in order to avoid the problem, and further, in its attempts to live "around" the problem that it ignores. The ignoring requires behaviors that are the hallmarks of dysfunction: denial, magical thinking, lies, and shame. When engaged in magical thinking, a person believes that their will and thoughts can make things real. Magical thinking is a bit like "where there's a will there's a way," yet absent of physical effort, regard for reality, or reasoning—a mad scientist without the science.

While it is most always more destructive and painful to postpone dealing with a problem than to face it constructively, conflict avoidance is a characteristic of dysfunctional families. Rationally, we all agree that letting our problems fester leads to a greater mess in the end; however, if we're in a dysfunctional family, we pretend things are fine—until things blow up. Even then, we attempt to bury, deny, and pretend.

In dysfunctional families, there is little value placed on what's true, including one's personal truth. As such, members of dysfunctional families will become cut off and isolated from extended family, friends, and society—all in order to avoid facing its problems. Healthy personal boundaries, respect, and compassion aren't practiced or modeled in dysfunctional homes. Instead, manipulation and shaming are practiced, and victim-perpetrator dynamics dominate.

GROWING UP IN A DYSFUNCTIONAL ENVIRONMENT

Dysfunctional childhood experiences cross class and cultural lines, and share common characteristics. In dysfunctional families, parents hold children and one another to perfectionist standards. Criticism is rampant—of the family members (and pets), as well as extended family and neighbors. So are fear and abuse. Emotions, feelings, and desires that don't align with the parents' wants or needs are rejected, shamed, or simply ignored.

Children growing up in dysfunctional environments tend to know—and feel responsible for—the emotions of the whole household. And some will even believe they have an impact on whether the family has a "good" day or a "bad" one. After all, if they are blamed for a day going badly, by the same logic, they must have the ability to prevent it. Growing up like this renders us chameleons, which can be both good and not so good.

The truth is, most of us knew more about our parents' emotional states and feelings than our own. Love is expressed conditionally in a dysfunctional home. This could mean that your parents praised, touched, and gave affection to you only if your behavior pleased them—but withheld it when that wasn't the case. It could mean that your parent noticed and valued only your appearance and attributed great meaning to it. For example, upon visiting, your parent might exclaim, "You look great!" and, satisfied that that's the whole of the story, proceed to talk about themselves without actually asking about your life or interior world.

Dysfunctional homes are wallpapered in fear. As a result, you may have been afraid of your parents, their moods, or their reactions because all of you existed in an environment laced with the threat of violence. And then there's the abuse you may have witnessed or endured, whether verbal, physical, or sexual. Whatever the shade of dysfunction you may have experienced and lived through, you are among friends here.

SETTING SAIL

After ten years of writing about self-healing for guesswhatnormalis.com, I became inspired to put together this book, which is to say, at long last. The inspiration came from my readers. They asked, again and again, "Where do I begin? How do I start the process of healing and doing the work of rewiring myself, of transforming my traumatic childhood?" So, here it is, my answer. This book is all about the beginning of healing. It's about saying "Hello, feelings" and regarding what you feel with compassion. It's about coaxing your Self —your true, inner, imperfect, and lovely Self—out into the light. It's about taking your own hand, being your own guide, and learning and growing through the act of investigating yourself. It's about getting to know who is really inside each of us and enticing that wonderful being out into the open more and more, bit by bit, with love.

We are sensitive beings, by nature. We're human animals. We adapt to situations and our survival is all important. If you grew up with parents who were unable to nurture you, then you did what any child does: you survived. You hid your needs if you sensed they were bothersome to your parent, focusing instead on theirs. If your needs were inconvenient, criticized, or doubted, maybe you acted as if you were strong or perfect, like everything was A-OK, hiding your natural right to vulnerability and your needs for help, guidance, and reassurance. Maybe you got the message that being "OK" was all that was acceptable, and understood deep down that being "OK" guaranteed your safety and security. That is what little beings do to survive. If that's anybody's fault, it's nature's.

Kindness toward yourself is the way out of pain, confusion, and doubt. I know this because I practice it every day. It's a way of life that doesn't cost a cent. Kindness toward yourself is a shift in thinking, a new habit that takes practice to form, and it's one that gives and gives and gives. Who knows? Perhaps your growth will inspire a few others around you to self-reflect, and by and by, your practice of self-kindness will lead to bigger change across your community, and even beyond that into the world surrounding all of us.

Survive or Die

For many years I assumed that the central trauma of my life was having an alcoholic father. In fact, not only did my father battle alcoholism, my mother did as well. My father got sober decades ago; my mother died suddenly at age 53 with a blood-alcohol level so high that she was comatose. And they, too, grew up with alcoholic parents—my dad's dad and my mom's mom, both of whom, puffed up and saturated, died from the disease of alcohol addiction. Alcoholism is "a family disease," not only because the drinking of one person in a family affects all members, but because it's usually an inherited addiction—through a combination of nature and nurture. Alcoholism is an addiction that courses through one's family tree for generations.

By growing up in an alcoholic family system, my ability to trust others became impaired. I say family "system" because when alcoholism is part of a family, it has its own power over the whole—you could say the entire family is under the influence, and that's true whether the alcoholic has become sober, or even if he or she still drinks.

It was my mother's abandonment of me when I was four years old that I now know to be the central trauma of my life. She simply chose not to raise me ("I set you free," she once told me with pride). Not only did she abandon me, but she didn't acknowledge that the abandonment had occurred. She left me with her parents for the weekend when I was three and a half years old and never returned except to visit occasionally. I often wondered if she expected me to "get over" her actions; her decision seeded in me a difficult-to-unearth trust handicap, knowing well how alcoholic family systems are full of lies and focused on appearances, perfectionism, and hyper-vigilance in order to cope with the unexpected mood changes and rages of the alcoholic. I also know well the sad possibility that a person, no matter how integrated in my life or committed to me by marriage or blood, can up and leave without explanation. It can happen; it did happen.

TRADING SURVIVAL LIVING FOR THRIVING

The words "journey" and "work" come to mind when I remember the first steps I took toward getting out of pain and into healing. In college, I first began to work on the issues that receiving poor parenting created for me. At the time, those issues were anxiety, lack of trust, and feeling on edge and peculiar. While I had been made to go to Alateen meetings in high school as my father started going to AA meetings, the meaning of my dad's alcoholism failed to click for me. I was still living at home, still in the inferno, surviving my alcoholic family. I wasn't in a position to see our family objectively in order to work on myself. But in college, after a breakup with a longtime boyfriend, I sensed that relationships were particularly hard for me—harder than for a normal person. As a result, I sought help. I found a therapist who taught me how to visualize my inner little girl and regard her feelings, and I would spend an hour or so after the sessions writing. I wrote pages and pages and pages, filling journal after journal.

Eventually, after college and some living of life followed by a graduate degree in creative writing, my writing began to transform into something that seemed useful to others like me. That writing—plus another decade of living, having a child, and carving out a career—became the blog guesswhatnormalis.com.

Without some gut instinct, writing, good therapy, and many self-help books, I might have taken the road that my childhood and family line had patterned for me—of codependence, addiction, and decision-making ruled by anxiety. Sometimes I wonder if breaking free means choosing a road that is tougher, lonelier, and scarier. Indeed the road to growth, freedom, and ourselves is an adventurous one.

Yet isn't it the only choice?

Your Journey

It is time to thrive. To get more joy out of your life, feel like yourself, and enjoy interactions with others, you must complete your growing-up process by your own hand. Whether you're in your 20s, your 80s, or somewhere in between, you likely can't believe you haven't yet done this work. Who cares?! Once you're on the journey, it won't matter why it began when it did. It might have been someone else's responsibility to raise you and prepare you for life better than they did, but you get to finish the job. You're the only one who can. And you get to do it your way. Regardless of your current age, beginning is all that matters.

How to Work Through the Book

I put this collection of activities together with a start-to-finish progression in mind; start from the beginning and work your way through to the end.

Every single activity in this book has potential to become the basis for an insight or healing experience for you. There are no forms to rush through and fill out here—you can regard each activity as its own world. Some may pack more of a punch for you today, depending on where you are in life, and others will resonate more for you at a later time. Utilize the pages and tools that resonate with you today.

The tools that have helped me along the way and that I have created this workbook around are: writing (journaling, blogging, and email exchanges), reflection, feeling, and reading. I have worked every one of these activities in this book because each was necessary—they are the result of how I approached the inquiry into myself, and of my healing work.

The Book's Four Parts

Part One: I Seek You

As you approach Part One of this book, the idea is to slow down and notice yourself: your mind and its thoughts. What—or who—is the source of those thoughts? Are those *your* thoughts? Do you like and agree with them, or are they old tapes from childhood? Regard yourself as an observer, an investigator—of You. Approach the activities as if you had a license to see, say, and feel anything; any feeling or thought that arises for you is valid.

Part Two: Feelings and Feeling Them

In this part, the idea is to identify, look at, and make friends with your feelings. If you grew up in a dysfunctional household, you're likely the product of the essential dysfunctional family motto (that's never said outright to family members, yet is always in operation): Don't Talk, Don't Think, Don't Feel. As you work through Part Two, the idea is to learn the language of feelings, try on what it's like to have a right to your feelings, and embrace them as normal, valid, and an A-OK part of what makes you *you*.

Part Three: Navigating Sabotage

When you get to Part Three, you'll go behind the scenes of sabotage and open the curtain to expose what's there—you'll see the mechanics of sabotage and how to disassemble it. As part of that, you'll be noticing the critic and saboteur in your mind, getting practice with rewriting the critic's script, and aiming love at your inner saboteur. You'll examine if you and time are in conflict, giving yourself an opportunity to contemplate time, find out the time things actually take, and coming to a place of respect and compassion for time.

Part Four: Caring for You

This part can be considered one giant hug—a big, luxurious hug that you can give yourself. These chapters are filled with ideas for self-care, spiritual practice, setting up a nurturing home environment, and sensing your personal rights. You will delve into a study of self-esteem, learning what it's composed of and how to strengthen it and lean on it, and how to take care of yourself through loving self-parenting. You'll also find ideas for making your environment a comforting one, knowing and honoring your needs, and enjoying and sharing yourself with the world.

The tools in this book are meant to support you in your growing-up and healing process. You *can* have a life in which you grow, feel alive and happy, and feel like yourself—and *like* yourself—while living at ease. Show kindness toward yourself, regard yourself with curiosity, and look openly and directly within yourself as you go forward.

I hope that you feel a sense of warm, calm love brewing up from
your belly to your heart as you work through these pages.
The act of doing this work creates its own magic.

PART ONE:
I Seek You

Beckon and Befriend
Your Inner Child

The most terrifying thing is to accept oneself completely.

—C. G. Jung

For every hero's journey there is a hero and his sidekick. For Luke Skywalker, it was Han Solo. For Frodo it was Samwise Gamgee. For you, it's actually *you*—your inner child.

To draw forth your inner child from the deep past requires a bit of quiet and patience. It isn't terribly different from sitting in a boat on a lake and fishing: observing patiently and with curiosity are the key elements.

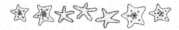

Sit comfortably, close your eyes, take a few breaths, and begin to imagine yourself as you were long, long ago, as a child.

Start by peering as far back as you can, imagining scenes from your childhood. Do this sequentially, beginning by picturing yourself as a baby in your crib, then slowly growing up ... perhaps walking, riding a bike, playing hide-and-and-go-seek, sitting on the classroom rug, then at your desk at school, riding a bus, setting up a fort in your closet, playing games with friends, feeling bored, being lost in your imagination ...

Let your mind travel around in time for a bit, then see if a particular moment from your childhood rises to the surface or catches your attention.

Now visualize yourself at the age you were when you may have first become aware of things being not quite right in your family, when you might remember a sense of unease, of feeling scared or vulnerable. Picture yourself then and there at that age. (For me, that moment occurred when I was six. I remember fights—one in which a door was slammed so hard that the paint along the edge of the molding split up and down like a jagged seam. I would look at that split seam over the years we lived in that house and always feel an emotional jolt.)

If you can't quite bring your inner child into focus, some prompts to consider are: What did you look like then? Can you visualize your hair, your face, your shoulders, your physique—or maybe your jacket or your shoes? Can you imagine being that small? Can you imagine what it felt like to be alive in your body as a child?

Once you have a visual, once you can see yourself as a child, reach out to that child and place your hand on its shoulder. Imagine yourself kneeling down, gazing into the eyes of yourself as a child, expressing that you're here to take care of him or her. You can say, "I'm here now. I've grown up and come back for you. I love you and I'm going to protect you today, and always."

Allow great compassion to pass from you to that child. Even though it may be difficult to face this innocent version of you, being compassionate and kind to your inner child is essential.

Keep this child in your heart. Allow yourself to have this visualized conversation with him or her whenever you like over the years—during tough times, brilliant ones, or whenever one of you needs it. I once had an unexpected conversation with my inner child during a deep freeze in Massachusetts. I was carefully picking my way around ice patches on the sidewalks while turning over a problem in my mind—a challenging personal situation that was calling for some maturity. My inner child popped into my mind, very suddenly and very clearly. I let her into the dialogue. "I'm deciding to grow up a bit," I said to her, "and I can see you're ready to do the same. I'll guide you through." I was talking to her, to myself, to both of us.

Making a Pledge to the Work

One way to embark on a healing journey is to say that the journey has begun, and to begin it with a gesture of kindness toward yourself. Making a pledge to yourself sets the tone for the work to come. It is hard like a promise and soft like a wish. A pledge to yourself makes it real and difficult to ignore or "forget" because it allows little room for doubt that you are in fact cultivating a new approach to life. The journey ahead is fortified by three aspects: intention, ceremony, and commitment.

Intention

Intention isn't only about what you hope to get out of this self-healing work, but the spirit in which you're doing it—the *why*. While you may hope to improve your marriage, for example, through this work, your deeper intention may actually be to achieve greater emotional intelligence. While you may hope to end up-and-down cycles of weight gain and loss, or of hope and hopelessness, your deeper intention may be to love yourself at any given moment, whether in struggle or ease.

Perhaps an event triggered this work for you—maybe an argument, a painful loss, or a breakup. Maybe it was merely some final-straw event when everything snapped into sharp focus, forcing you to find a more effective approach to life, even if you had little foresight into what that approach would look like. Or, perhaps you simply—finally—*get* it and realize that you do matter, that you truly count, and that you intend to finally start putting yourself first (or at least not last all the time).

Think now about your intention. Stop here and take a few moments to consider it—write a few notes, or take a walk around the block and let your intention for this work rise to a fully-formed conscious thought. You may want to learn how to identify and feel comfortable with your feelings, to manage anger, to express your needs and wants to your partner and family, to learn to handle criticism with grace, or to feel good about yourself during good times and bad. Whatever your intention is, name it.

CEREMONY

Ceremony transforms healing into something both playful and transcendent—and memorable. Ceremony also has the function of slowing us down a few beats, allowing our deepest intentions to sink in and be facilitated by physical action. You might think of the word "ceremony" as something involving funerals or weddings, or rituals of medieval times involving cauldrons and fire. But ceremony is little more than a series of steps, a procedure, or a format for doing something. In writing this book, my ceremony involved setting out a few books by writers I admire, as well as index cards, my journal, pens, and pencils, and standing at my workspace and taking a deep, mind-clearing breath before I began to sketch out what this book would be.

Ceremony is a ritual that sets habits in place, permitting you, over time, to begin your work without having to agonize over it or browbeat yourself into getting started. Work that begins with ceremony becomes habit as you look forward to it, and to how things will proceed after it.

You may want to turn off your phone, lock the door, and fill a glass with water as your ceremony. Or you could tell those around you that you're going to be doing some "work" and need to be left alone for thirty minutes, and then change into comfortable clothes. Another ceremony could be to sit and take in five deep breaths before opening a notebook you have chosen to use only for your self-healing work. Being present as you ready yourself—perhaps by stretching, closing your eyes, lighting a candle, meditating, or brewing tea—is really all you need to do.

I have turned out lights and lit candles as part of scene setting for writing work; I've crafted inspiration boards and created certificates of self-regard and permission for myself as part of my healing work. The steps need not be rigidly followed—depending on the day, your mood, and the work, the steps will be different. Maybe you have an urge to hold a stone in the palm of your hand—great, doing that alone creates ceremony. A few other ideas could be:

* Heading out to the garage in comfortable shoes, turning on the light and some jazz music, unlocking your tools, and saying "time to create!" while pulling the cover off the motorcycle you're restoring.

* Waking early, putting on thick socks, checking on your sleeping children, splashing water onto your face, then sitting and meditating.

* Brushing your teeth, stretching, and doing a few push-ups before settling into research and note-taking about unmanned space exploration vehicles.

When you take a break during your work, consider remaining connected or somehow engaged by carrying a part of your project with you, keeping the spirit of it alive; take an object, page of writing, piece of fabric, or list onto the couch or into the hammock with you while you rest.

You decide to rest a bit . . . and so you put chisel and mallet back in the toolbox. The second your fingers abandon the tool, the chisel returns to cold steel; the mallet goes back to being a mere wooden assembly . . . You have abandoned them, they now abandon you . . . To let go of the tools of your trade, to exit the theater of your creating during a pause, is to annihilate the entire meaningful alchemy you have created in your practice.

—Philippe Petit, Creativity

COMMITMENT

There's that word. *Commitment.* We are ambivalent about commitment. Why? Because when we commit to a plan, it seems to allow so little room for a sense of control, so little freedom in the event we need to jump up and escape, to run for our lives.

Yet commitment is simply a foothold, something to anchor you and keep you steady while you work. Just as the next rung on a ladder steadies you as you decide whether to climb further up or jump off, a commitment is a type of home base or point of balance from which to move—or to live. There is a greater amount of room to move within the framework of commitment than we suppose; it provides stability for deeper experience. A commitment is a pledge.

I invite you to make a pledge to your self-healing.

In writing your pledge, you may want to simply write it on the next page. Yet it doesn't have to stop there. You may also feel moved to type it into a note-taking app on your phone, compose a song about yourself, or create an artistic collage that expresses your declaration of healing. Perhaps you'll want to use colored pencils, even if for the first time in decades, and decorate your Pledge of Self-Healing. You decide. But whatever you write, let it be with yourself—and your inner child—in mind, and full of love and compassion. Make it a big deal and full of intention.

Here's mine:

Pledge of Self-Healing

I, Amy Eden, promise to love the child within me, the child who endured, adapted, and survived. That child deserves my love, kindness, respect, and nurturing. I hereby commit to provide that compassion to myself. I will accept myself. I will cherish my faults. I will be Home to myself. I will love myself, just as I am today and any given day.

PLEDGE of SELF-HEALING

I PLEDGE ALLEGIANCE to myself

Catching Your Thoughts

Your mind is the garden, your thoughts are the seeds,
the harvest can either be flowers or weeds.

—William Wordsworth

I used to believe self-esteem was all about saying, "no." I thought it was about setting and upholding personal boundaries. But self-esteem is so much more than that—it's the product of instinct + action. It's a verb. You can think of instinct as a gut sense and action as what you do in reaction to your gut sense. Put both to use. Instinct and action are a powerful and fertile combination.

I educated myself about self-esteem through reading a lot of self-help books, many of which I've listed at the back of this book, and through exploring what it feels like to be lacking in it—that is, dealing with the fallout of not behaving with my self-esteem on board. Yet it was through action that I really got it, by acting from what kept me even-keeled, which was my self-esteem. Thank goodness self-esteem grows! By this I mean that you don't have to ignite it again and again once the pilot light is "on." Self-esteem grows like plants do: feed it and get it into some sunlight, and as long as you nurture it fairly consistently, it shocks you by actually blossoming, growing, and strengthening. Once cultivated, you never have to start self-esteem from seed again.

If you grew up in my house as a child, you would have heard a lot of criticism of other people. Anyone. Everyone. The neighbors? Lazy. Your aunt? Heathen. Your uncle? Selfish. Grandparents? Judgmental. Cousins? Undereducated. Friends of the family? Too ambitious. And on, and on. It wasn't just criticism of their behavior that I heard ("The neighbor forgot to pull her trash bins off the sidewalk *again*"), but the criticism bled into the personality and moral fiber of the person as well, as attacks of character: "She can't take two seconds to pull her bins off the curb? I can only wonder what the inside of her house looks like. She probably can't pay her bills on time either. Her childhood must have been really bad."

If you heard your parents criticize others, you most likely knew well the actions that were disapproved of, and you probably tried to avoid doing the types of things you'd heard criticized. As you grew up, you may have learned to turn their criticism (imagined and real) onto yourself. I inherited this brand of ugliness and grew up aiming the mean criticisms I had overheard during my childhood at myself and, unfortunately, at others too. If I didn't pay my rent on time, I'd think I was deeply flawed and headed for self-sabotage, rather than that I was simply distracted by changing jobs that month and *forgot*. Humans forget things, right? Humans are imperfect, right? Yet if we have forgotten to pull our garbage bins off the street after the garbage is collected, rather than think, "I'm exhausted. I'll grab those in the morning," we think, "If I can't handle taking two seconds to drag the trash bins off the curb, how am I ever going to succeed at anything?" You'll out your sorry self to the neighbors too, not that they don't already suspect you're lazy. (Why take yourself down a notch when you can destroy yourself down to your core?) We can deal ourselves killer blows with a single thought. We were raised to. It is learned self-brutality.

Not only do we tend to think brutal thoughts about our deepest selves, but we also connect dots that shouldn't be connected as part of that style of self-criticism. For example, the way I grew up, I learned to think of certain actions as related to one another: trash cans and success, for example. Somehow I believed that taking in trash cans could be related to being a successful person. That's darned unhelpful and a terrifying way to move through life, not to mention flat-out wrong.

Catching Your Thoughts

How do you begin to catch your inner critic mid-grumble? How do you compassionately listen to and negotiate with an unruly committee of the mind? The first step is to catch your thoughts in action by listening in to them, slowing down, and deciding to be an observer of yourself; then really noticing how you think, what you think, and observing your mind.

Not all thoughts are the same types. Some are random, quick reactions to a small event —such as when you eat a second piece of cake when you didn't plan to. Others are decades-old thoughts that lurk or hang around—such as when you think about looking for a new job or starting a project—that rise up and influence you. Others still are anxiety-like thoughts—such as the ones that strike in the middle of the night or give you a tight, queasy stomach first thing in the morning.

Consider your first, waking thoughts of the day. To what does your mind first jump? Is it that you have to go to *that job*? Is it *the commute*? Is it that *you're still late on that overdue project*? Is it remembering that yesterday you put off an important personal goal *once again*? Or the waking realization that you're *still in that relationship* you were going to end? Or that you didn't magically wake up as *the-painter-who-sells-paintings* you so badly want to be? Downer thoughts aren't limited to the moment you wake up, but it can be a good time to discover them. Our waking thoughts tend to be raw, honest, and closer to our subconscious. As we wake, we are (at least for a moment) free of layers of false selves.

In truth, our layers of false selves aren't as opaque as we think; our masks are rather transparent. What we tell others we are does not impress, alter, or control what others see, though we would like to think the opposite is true. Similarly, what others tell us they are, they may or (likely not) may not be. I remember once saying something to the effect of, "For every mask you don, I just see you more clearly," to a man who favored phrases that began with, "I'm the kind of guy ..."

Yet masks aren't undesirable. While they may often be mistaken for the entirety of an identity, masks are essential tools for wading through society, making our way through the day, and expressing our humanhood.

For we are revealed not only as our disguises slip or are abandoned but in the nature of the disguises we choose. Pretenses are always insufficient, overcompensatory, or both. Masks melt into our faces and become impossible to remove precisely at the instant we realized they were transparent all along.

— Jonathan Lethem, The Disappointment Artist

For an example, what thoughts do you have about your after-work routine? Do you leave work on time? Is it a struggle? Do you make any time for sitting quietly once home? What about your weekends? Your friends and social life? And your way of feeding yourself? All situations and times of day are fair game and ripe for self-study.

Here are some sample thoughts:

I hate this. I'm always rushed in the morning and it's like I can't escape the cycle. It's clearly simpler for other people. I can't just get up when the alarm clock buzzes.

I need too much alone time—I can't get enough. I shouldn't need so much time to myself. Seems like I'd probably have more of a social life and be a better friend if I got out more.

I want to eat cookies. I wish I didn't. I wish I had the self-control of a normal person. I'm stressed. I'm too old for food cravings, aren't I? I've got to be sexy again.

Write down as many as you can on the next page. Don't worry about sounding whiny or ungrateful, just be accurate. What are you frustrated about? Jealous of? What do you secretly want? What's distracting your mind? What thoughts, wishes, or worries are bumming you out? Record your thoughts honestly. Will they sound silly? Will they surprise you? Yes and yes. Is that normal? Yes. Do you have to show this to anyone? No!

Observe your thoughts with curiosity. Make notes about the unhelpful, automatic thoughts and the negativity and dread that goes on in your mind. Write down what you hear yourself think about yourself. Continue to slow down and observe your thoughts for a few weeks. The more practice you get at this, the easier it becomes to lure, hook, and catch the thoughts, and eventually, toss them right back into the water.

Once you've recorded a few caught thoughts, see if you can spot and then rewrite a few of them. And this time, *emphasize* their absurdities. By "absurdity" I mean unfair comparisons, nonsense, and false logic, as well as silly, victim-y, and unlikely consequences.

Taking my caught-thought examples from before, here they are with exaggeration and the absurdities glorified:

Every morning, rush, rush, rush because you never get up on time. Hell-o, I guess you don't want to be successful. Because honestly all you have to do is jump out of bed when the alarm clock buzzes!

I need sooooo much alone time, too much—a freakish amount. I should move to a cabin in the woods. I'd be a better friend and have a social life if I didn't need all this time to process, think, and feel everything!

I'm a Cookie Monster who can't get enough. Normal people eat, like, two cookies. I can eat them till I'm ill. I wasn't meant to be a sexy woman because if I were, I would have been born without a sweet tooth and with some self-control!

Taking things to the extreme like this can help you get some distance and to laugh at yourself a bit. Sometimes when dealing with our thoughts, it can be therapeutic to go for drama, to ratchet up pathetic to an extreme—and in so doing, face fears. Try it on the next page.

Are you curious what your thoughts reveal about how your mind works? Are you curious about what your underlying wishes, longings, and frustrations are? The process of investigating your thoughts involves capture and study. You've done a bit of capturing, so now you can study what you've caught.

INVESTIGATING YOUR THOUGHTS

Consider the thoughts you wrote down on the first journal page. Choose one that seems simple, that contains a straightforward or mundane woe, like going to bed too late, skipping brushing your teeth, not returning someone's call, or not filling your gas tank before it hits empty. Then explore it, in writing, by posing questions to yourself about the situation.

Questions you might pose to yourself:

* Would it be the worst thing if I kept doing this?

* What does it say about me that I do this?

* Does it *really* say that about me?

* How do I feel when this happens?

* Why do I feel that way?

* Am I judging myself unfairly?

* What might be the reasons I do this?

* What if I learned that brilliant, beautiful, famous, and rich people do this too?

* What would I say to my inner child if he or she did that?

* What is the most compassionate way I can respond to myself here?

* Is there a problem here, or am I being hard on myself?

* Is there another way to see this?

Those are just starter questions. Try what fits. Once you start asking fitting questions of yourself, you'll know it because the thoughts will just flow. Truly. Simply start writing questions to yourself, and the rest will follow.

Here's my dialogue-in-writing, using the thought I caught about time alone ("I need too much alone time—I can't get enough. I shouldn't need so much time to myself. Seems like I'd probably have more of a social life and be a better friend if I got out more."):

What would be the worst thing about meeting up with a friend for coffee even if I was totally exhausted? Why do I think I have to be well-rested in order to go meet up with friends? Is that not perfectionist thinking? Do things really have to be "just right" in order for me to go have fun? I always thought perfectionism was about work performance, and I never really considered it could show up in this kind of way. I act like things have to be "just right," but I don't actually believe that when I stop to think about it. Why don't I take more time by myself? What if I took two hours to myself and saw what it felt like? Do I feel like I will "fall apart" or fail to uphold some kind of "persona" if I'm not able to have time to myself before sharing my time with others? Do I judge myself for needing time by myself? Is it really true that I need more time to myself than any other person? Is it possible I'm judging myself overly harshly here, holding myself to some kind of standard I'm unaware of? Is it possible that this is a case of needing a "normal" amount of time to myself but for some reason I feel guilty about it? I remember that whenever I was sitting idle while I was growing up, my father would give me a project to do, so maybe the guilt about time to daydream or read stems from that. I'd rather feel balanced than guilty, and I don't actually think there's anything wrong with taking time by myself. In fact, what I actually truly believe is that it's essential to being a conscious person and a writer! And when I look at how full my days are, I have to admit that there's really no time to myself in there, so of course I'm craving it. I bet that even thirty minutes a day would really turn things around ...

The ideal mind frame for this thought investigation activity is curiosity, to simply wonder what might be going on with you and to be open to where the questions and their answers might lead.

Your turn. Choose one of your caught thoughts and question it in writing below.

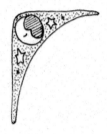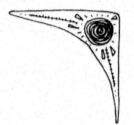

I hope you're starting to sense, through writing about your thoughts and starting a dialogue with yourself, that you are growing the ability to heal yourself by your own hand.

A DEEPER CONTEMPLATION

But wait—there's still more to consider. The final step is to go even deeper by studying and contemplating what you just wrote. Think of it as finding wallpaper under a painted wall, getting curious about what color is beneath, and peeling back layer after layer with questions. Take a look at what you wrote on the previous page and notice words, phrasing, and tone. Ask questions of your writing, such as:

* Does that word choice or phrasing sound like me or someone else?

* Is there a conflict between what I think I'm *supposed* to do and what I *want* to do?

* What kinds of assumptions are at play?

* What is my greatest fear in this situation?

* If I don't actually believe this, what's the origin of this thought?

* What's at risk if I choose not to think this way?

When you hit on a realization or get to the underlying feelings, expectations, or beliefs fueling your thoughts, you'll know it. You'll feel it. And then you'll have arrived at something you can work with, because you'll have hit the point from which you can rewrite what you think.

Working through this activity is an act of kindness toward yourself. Welcome feelings of love—and great relief—that well up inside you (the real you) as you work through these questions. Write your thoughts on the next page.

Every. Single. Pain and Loss

I imagine one of the reasons people cling to their hates so stubbornly is because they sense,
once hate is gone, they will be forced to deal with pain.

—James Baldwin

We are marked by our wounds. We think this is a burden, an embarrassment, a curse. It is not. How we choose to live in relation to our wounds creates our story. The wounds we don't choose; the story, however, we write.

Have you ever noticed that you tend to feel bad when you remember certain wrongs that were done to you in the past? They simply come to mind and—zing!—give you a pinch? Do you sometimes then rehash the whole thing, again (and again)? Have you ever thought to count up how many different instances of those wrongs, resentments, pains, and losses you have pinging you from the past? Would you believe that my grandmother's disgust at my gummy smile and her calling me a homely child defined my feelings about my appearance for *years*? True story. This is your chance to record each of the pains, losses, resentments, and complaints about the stuff that's happened to you—since birth (or heck, *before* birth—should you actually resent something that occurred in utero, go for it!).

Write down *everything*.

We carry around stories about our pain that we seldom stop to conduct a fresh investigation of. Your emotional landscape contains emotional wounds. For some, there will be old physical wounds as well. These may be few or many, and they may be deep and surprisingly painful. As we go about our way in the world, our wounds are with us, more present and influential than you'd guess.

I love this tool—it's adapted from an empowerment seminar I once attended and offers a rare opportunity to vent, to be heard (by you), and to make a record of the things that hurt but can't be expressed, either because you have already expressed them, perhaps over and over, or because somewhere along the line you decided the situation was merely too old and historical to still be complaining about. When you work with this tool, no hurt is off limits, too small, or too old. The key is to capture them all, each and every pain, each and every loss.

You will be surprised, and you will also be unburdened.

The idea isn't to shed or resolve these pains and losses, by the way. The point here is to collect them all and do a complete audit of your emotional landscape. That's enough! So just as you might record each of your expenses as part of taking stock of why you're coming up overdrawn at month's end, you're collecting data about the feelings that take a toll on you emotionally. And so, "Where's my money being spent?" becomes "Where's my emotional energy being spent?"

There are all kinds of pains and losses. Some that have appeared on my list are:

Being abandoned by my mother
Moving away from my grandparents' house
Having to let my stepmother adopt me
Being bullied and teased in fourth grade
The word-of-mouth breakup my first day of high school
Losing my best friend to a different group of friends

Being told I was a homely child

My best friend not writing me any more letters

Loving an addict

Having my job relocated back to Boston

Giving up my cats

My mother's death

The loss of a relationship that was supposed to be lifelong

Not having another child

Getting older

Enduring my partner withdrawing from me

Another person's list might look like this:

My brother burning my teddy bear

Not getting picked for basketball

Mom not caring that my quilt didn't cover my cold feet

Getting teased in 5th grade

When Blackie died

Dad's affair

Having to choose between my parents

My coach hitting me

Always being expected to get A's like I was an academic robot

My business partner backing out

Nobody said goodbye when I moved across the country

You can apply this exercise in a multitude of ways over time. For example, you can create a pains and losses list specific to your birthday, or to family vacations or the holidays. Writing a pains and losses list is a tool to use over and over, especially at difficult times in your life.

Ready? Write down each and every pain and loss you've experienced, ever. Big or small.

*   *

*   *

*   *

*   *

*   *

*   *

*   *

*   *

*   *

*   *

*   *

*   *

*   *

Don't be surprised if you feel like a gutted fish after pouring out your pains and losses. It can be overwhelming to recount every single life tragedy, big and small. When I wrote my first list of pains and losses, two things surprised me: how quickly the items came to me and how short the list was. I thought I would need an hour to write them all down, and yet it took about fifteen minutes.

There is great value in writing down an exhaustive list of your pains and losses. It provides you with an opportunity to be a witness to your own hurts, and it enables you to honor those pains and losses, without worrying about how insignificant or old another person might consider them. It also gives you an opportunity to lighten the weight those losses hold through the act of naming them.

At the Bottom of the Ocean

What if you regarded your list of pains and losses *and* your caught thoughts, together? What might you discover by juxtaposing them? Might there actually be something to see —such as correlations between your caught thoughts and your losses?

Although the list of your pains and losses probably includes some old hurts and your caught thoughts are likely more recent, we tend to hold the past close. So despite the years between them, it's likely that the unfinished business of our past wounds are alive and well —and expressed—in our present thoughts.

When I juxtapose my pains and losses and caught thoughts, what do I see? What I notice first is a theme of rejection. The rejection of my mother deciding not to raise me, the rejection of my best friend no longer writing me letters, and the rejection of being broken up with on the first day of high school. I can appreciate how that kind of rejection—unexplained and sudden— could lead me to feel uncertain about myself and my worth as a person. When I take another look at my list of pains and losses, I see things that happened to me and that affected me deeply, and all were events over which I had no control. That's a terrifying combination.

Given that, it seems pretty natural to me that perfectionism would come into play for me in adulthood, that I might battle perfectionism as emotional "logic"—that is, the "logic" that if I'm perfect and if what I create is perfect, then it *cannot* be rejected or abandoned.

My lesson, then, is to understand that perfectionism is a trap, a farce. Striving for perfection is to travel an isolated road toward a destination that not only continually recedes, but doesn't exist.

If you weren't shown loving acceptance that instilled a deeply rooted sense of self, it's now time to give that to yourself, as well as to give it to others. It flows back and forth. In his book *The Mastery of Love*, Don Miguel Ruiz writes this about "right" romantic partners and the ability to not only recognize that but honor it: "You are going to be the right man for her if she loves you just the way you are and she doesn't want to change you." Put another way: you are the right person for yourself, and should love yourself, as you are right now and not as a result of who you'll become.

Dive for the Pearl

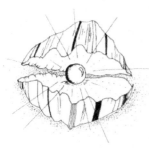

What surprises or emotional "logic" do you see when you step back and examine your juxtaposed list and thoughts? Take time to consider it. Deep work doesn't need to be rushed and in fact benefits from your taking time with the investigation. You are learning to lead an examined, courageous life. What do you see? Write it all down on the following page.

Humbly Seeing Three Sides to the Story

Humility is not thinking less of yourself, it's thinking of yourself less.
—C.S. Lewis

I believe humility is a deep strength. It requires—and tests—our comfort level with believing in our worth while regarding that same worth as equal to all things. I do mean *all* things in the universe. When we can regard all as equal, we can hear one another. And if you can know that your truth is valid while appreciating the different truth of another person—and even truths and perspectives that perplex you—true, vital compassion is achieved.

Tonglen, for one example, is a Tibetan healing practice that I once read about in an article by Thich Nhat Hanh in *Shambala* magazine. The power of it (once I tried it) absolutely blew me away. *Tonglen* involves focusing on the pain or ailment of another person (that stranger who dropped then stepped on his eyeglasses crossing the street) while inhaling that pain—into you. As you exhale, you then push joy or hope or some positive feeling their way. (I know, it sounds too simple. And maybe it sounds like you can "catch" their problem by breathing in their ailment; however, as soon as you try it, you'll see how absurd that worry is.) It's a beautiful practice that cultivates self-compassion in a surprisingly generous way—through directing your compassion outward.

Might you be game to uproot a couple of those ancient pains and dissolve them? This next activity will guide you through how to do that. The first time you use this tool, you may want to choose a situation that has a weak hold on you, rather than something blindingly evocative. Once you have a feel for how to use the tool, go on to tackle deeper conflicts.

OPPORTUNITIES FOR RESOLUTION

Is there a particular item from your pains and losses list that you're ready to resolve, or may be willing to consider potentially resolving?

You can use this writing exercise to see things from different perspectives—three of them —by composing three unique accounts of a situation. The first account is from your perspective (who you were at the time), the second is from the other person's perspective (as they were in that time and place), and the third is from a neutral outsider's point of view. Now, there's no knowing what the other person thought, but this is an opportunity to practice seeing with others' eyes, putting yourself in another person's shoes, and considering their point of view.

While it's tempting to choose a loss that's more evocative, urgent, and present-day, I've instead chosen a long-ago pain as an example—my best friend ceasing to write letters to me when we were thirteen—because it illustrates how very long I carried the pain.

My Perspective

I was hurt when Mona stopped writing to me because I felt rejected and confused. I wasn't sure exactly what it was that I wrote in my last letter that caused her never to write back, but I remember feeling like she was bragging about her life and I'd addressed that in my letter. I was worried that I came off as scolding her. Actually, what I was most worried about was that she rejected me for my insecurity and for getting emotional with her. I never knew. Maybe she was really mad, really offended. I'll never know because she didn't say anything one way or the other. I just wished she'd forget about the letter and write to me.

My Friend's Perspective

Amy sent me a letter preaching to me about "sharing" rather than "comparing" our lives, and it was confusing and annoying. Could I say it was even downright bitchy? Why couldn't she be excited for me and understand that I would never brag to her? After all, we are—or were—best friends. And after all, *she* was the one who left. I guess life in California is changing her. I'll see if she writes again to apologize, and then we'll take it from there.

An Outsider's Perspective

TIP: Think of this as writing a story in which you and the other person are characters, so you can't know anything about what's going on in either person's mind; therefore, you must keep it stripped down to *actions* and *facts* alone.

Amy and Mona lived in Minnesota and were best friends in fifth and sixth grade, and then in the middle of sixth grade, Amy's family moved to California. Mona made new friends after Amy left. And Amy made friends in her new school too. They wrote letters to each other over the months, and at one point the letters stopped. Amy had written the last letter, which went unanswered.

But Vent First

Before I could craft the three versions, I needed to get the raw, subjective, emotional, version out first, like this:

> She was selfish to cut me out. I'm human. We're friends. Couldn't she have gotten over a dumb comment? Couldn't she see past jealousy and just get back on track with our friendship? Was I jealous? Was she jealous? Was I totally rude to her and blind to it? Was she just waiting for an excuse to cut me out of her life? Why not at least tell me to go to hell first? What happened?!

What I love most about this exercise is that it's not at all about who is in the right vs. who is in the wrong. That's not a part of it. The sole goal is to represent the various perspectives. There's freedom in releasing ourselves from that common trap. Our culture, as well as our families, tend to want to put people and actions into neat "Bad" and "Good" canisters on the wall, but are people and our actions really that simple and one-dimensional? Hardly.

For me, stepping outside of right and wrong is key. Right and wrong is just another version of the black and white type of rigid and conditional thinking that I'd rather put way, way behind me. Coming to a place of seeing the various perspectives that coexist is a step beyond the playground, a step toward grace and a part of maturity.

This exercise is a challenge, but eye-opening too. There is something about writing about the issue from the other person's point of view that helps to get as close as possible to walking in their shoes. This process takes a bit of the sting out of the emotional intensity. Once you actually write down the words that express how the other person may have seen it, it's impossible not to feel compassion for him or her.

First, write out the situation below with raw, resentful, and unedited emotion.

Next, as you compose the three perspectives of the situation, remember this: different and opposing perspectives coexist in life. There is no ultimate wrong/right or bad/good. As you write how things transpired from your perspective, consider:

✳   How, exactly, did you behave and what, exactly, did you say?

✳   What did you do, or say, that made sense to you but might have been misinterpreted?

✳   What did you secretly desire, but not express?

While you may not know what the other person truly and actually thought, you can use all that you know to make your best guess. Take care with considering the situation while standing in their shoes.

* What kind of words would you use to capture the voice of the other person?

* From where did the person come, or situation arise, that could inform how they'd describe it?

* Giving them the *benefit of the doubt*, how might they have meant the best in their own way?

Now, finally, describe the scene, conversation, or situation in a strictly factual way, noting only what could be witnessed, and actually seen:

* If you were to observe the situation out of earshot, how would you describe it based on body language?

* How would you describe the interaction or situation as a 90-year-old person at the end of your life?

* How would you write the scene in a screenplay for a movie or stage play?

MAYBE WE'RE BOTH RIGHT

Read over what you wrote. Regard your feelings, noticing whether they have shifted, lifted, or changed completely since you viewed the situation in new ways. How tough was it to imagine it from the other person's point of view? Did you have to battle pride or ego in order to do so? What was at stake for you in stepping into the other person's shoes?

Some other questions to consider:

* What's in the way of your letting this go?

* What do you still want from the situation?

* On what assumptions are your feelings based?

* What don't you know about this situation?

After doing this exercise myself, I had the realization that I had taken the road of inaction. I'd waited and waited, wanting to get a letter from my friend. I expected her to make the next move, and it never occurred to me to write her another letter out of turn, to not wait for her to reciprocate. I had every reason to make the next move—to write to her, to apologize, own my words, check in about whether there was, indeed, a miscommunication or hurt feelings. Instead, I just waited and grew more resentful that she wasn't writing to me. Not only that, but I carried around the pain and loss with me for years!

That was not the last time I took the road of inaction and stirred it into a pot with resentment. In retrospect, I cringe when I realize that I've done the inaction/resentment thing plenty of times.

Your turn, courageous one. Write about your insights on the following page.

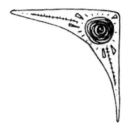

We have to accept ourselves in order to write.
Now none of us does that fully; few of us do it even halfway.
Don't wait for one hundred percent acceptance of yourself before you write,
or even eighty percent acceptance. Just write.
The process of writing is an activity that teaches us about acceptance.

—Natalie Goldberg

Greetings, Feelings

Hoping a situation will change keeps you at a distance from your true feelings—sadness, anger, fear. Each of these feelings is best appreciated up close. Feel them deeply, and they will cease to bother you. Hope they'll go away, and they'll bother you all day.

—Gay Hendricks

Feelings are like ocean waves. What do waves do? They rise, roll in, then roll away again. Some, no matter how firmly planted your feet are in the sand, will knock you backward or suck you into the depths. Other waves are tame, enjoyable, and unobtrusive to our equilibrium. Waves always come. Waves always recede. These are the facts.

Try to observe the waves more and fear them less. You can be unafraid of a feeling's potential to overpower you when you understand its nature: it rises, it rolls in, and then it goes. When you can be an observer of your feelings, they can do their thing—roll in, lap at your body, then recede—and you can do yours, without being toppled.

Being "emotional" is too often a criticism. People throw the phrase—cloaked as insult—at loved ones: "Don't get all emotional!" But, aren't our emotions what make us human? Don't our emotions prove that we're alive? Without emotions could we live a truly fulfilled life, know love, and feel inspired?

Is there a difference between feelings and emotions? Yes and no. Emotion is a general term, referring to a state of being; *emotional* is a big, general feeling throughout your body and mind that's unspecific. When someone says they're emotional, they're expressing a raw, general state of emotional vulnerability. *Feelings*, however, are more singular, specific, and easily labeled: excited, angry, hopeful, satisfied, and sleepy are a few.

Feelings have both mental and bodily aspects. For example, your mind may be on fire with anger and your forearms may be tight. If you were to observe, "I'm feeling mad," you'd be labeling a feeling, being specific. If you were to say, "I'm emotional," you're making a more general statement about your state of being. With an emotional state there's room to ask yourself the follow-up question, *What exactly am I feeling?* And that leads to being able to label feelings and communicate about them.

In becoming someone who can own their feelings but not be ruled by them, the first step is to have compassion for your feelings. The second step is to honor, allow, and simply feel those feelings. They won't envelop you, won't make you combust, quit your job, or run screaming through the streets. Once you experience compassion for your feelings and allow them in yourself, you will see that you're in charge because you understand how feelings function—you take the reins the moment you become unafraid of what you feel.

THE BIG LIST OF FEELINGS

Y ou are capable of having feelings that are big, small, surprising, and complex, as well as common and universal—more feelings than any list can contain. Underline the feelings listed here that might feel uncomfortable for you, and circle the ones you long to experience more of. Feel free to add words not listed here that apply to you.

Able	Aroused	Capable	Discouraged
Acceptance	Ashamed	Captivated	Distracted
Accepted	Awed	Carefree	Distraught
Adventurous	Awkward	Competitive	Dread
Affectionate	Beautiful	Content	Duped
Alive	Blissful	Courageous	Embarrassed
Amped	Blue	Creative	Enchanted
Angry	Bold	Crushed	Energetic
Anticipation	Bored	Curious	Energized
Anxious	Calm	Delighted	Envious

Excited	Hungry	Playful	Spiteful
Exhausted	Imaginative	Pouty	Stimulated
Exposed	Inspired	Powerful	Stuffed
Fearful	Introspective	Quiet	Talkative
Firm	Irritable	Raw	Thirsty
Flighty	Jealous	Sad	Tired
Foolish	Jumpy	Satisfied	Touched
Fried	Justified	Scared	Trapped
Giddy	Light	Seen	Traumatized
Glad	Lonely	Sexy	Understood
Gleeful	Longing	Shocked	Vulnerable
Happy	Loved	Shy	Weary
Heard	Nervous	Sleepy	Weepy
Honored	Numb	Small	Worried
Humble	Nurtured	Sneaky	Worthy

Trawling for Your Feelings

I learned to be with myself rather than avoiding myself with limiting habits;
I started to be aware of my feelings more, rather than numb them.
I learned to honor my feelings and go toward them rather than running away.
—Judith Wright

Why are the simplest answers hard to come by? When we're asked how we feel or even ask ourselves how we feel, too often we don't have a clue. We can't match words to our frustration or anger, or we don't know that we're angry because we were not allowed that feeling when we were growing up. We're numb. We're speechless. We are unpracticed in the art of feeling and navigating feelings.

And yet, feeling a feeling is simply that. To experience a feeling is to notice and acknowledge it—the feeling called embarrassment, the feeling called glee, or the feelings of hunger, impatience, or anger. You are not the feeling itself, nor do you have to identify as the feeling, react to it, or fix it. You only have to *feel* it.

Sit comfortably and close your eyes or let your gaze fall straight ahead on nothing in particular. Begin to breathe slowly and completely so that you breathe in through your nose and fill your diaphragm, belly, and lungs with your breath, and then exhale slowly through your mouth. Notice your breath; follow it as it travels through your body, as it flows in and down, builds and then climbs out. Continue like this, breathing slowly and gently for a while—two or three minutes or so—until you become a person who has given up every worry or concern in this moment and is focused solely on your breathing.

Begin to take a slow inventory of how your body feels. Does anything itch? How do your body and its muscles feel? Do you notice any tightness or pain anywhere? Is there any tension around your forehead, temples, eyes, or scalp? Take a slow inventory of your body, from your head to your fingertips and toes, and see what physical sensations you notice.

Before you go on, you may want to pause for a moment if feelings of fear or panic are rising in you. That's normal for some people, so don't be alarmed. If you feel resistance to this breathing exercise, that's normal too, especially if you've never tried it before. When you're ready to resume it, begin breathing again, and go from there. It's all part of the practice.

Next, begin to allow the emotions and feelings inside you to reveal themselves. Permit any feeling that arises, but only notice it—don't feed into it. Avoid thinking about particular situations related to that feeling; instead, just feel each feeling and nothing more. Loneliness might arise, or anguish, or fear, or longing, or confusion, or disorientation, or anger. Allow those feelings to be present. There's no need to problem-solve or resolve issues right now.

Remember the goal is not to fix, but merely to feel. Borrow one of these mottos to remember this approach: *Feel, don't fix* or *Feeling is fixing.* The only thing you need to do in this moment is observe and feel feelings that are inside of you, no matter how strong, varied, or inexplicable.

Continue to breathe and experience your feelings as you breathe. Then ask yourself the following questions of each feeling you notice and write down your answers.

What am I feeling?

Example: "I feel a lot of tightness and tiredness. Aches in my body. And hope. And fear. I've got worry. And a bit of anguish. But there's glee and love, too."

Where in my body do I feel that feeling?

Example: "I feel it in different spots. The love or hope is in my chest and belly, and that glee feeling is behind my eyes."

If you feel anxiety, where do you feel it?

Example: "The anxiety shows up in my forearms, lungs, and chest. At night it's in my jaw."

The next question to ask, while still breathing and observing your feelings with love and curiosity, is:

How does the sensation feel in my body?

Example: "My neck feels like something solid and heavy pressing down, plus a sharp pinching sensation. In my lungs the feeling is like a burning sensation."

Allow great compassion to pass through you, paying special attention to each of your organs—especially your heart and stomach—and extend to yourself deep kindness and any amount of love you're ready to offer yourself. If you are questioning whether this compassion-feeling is easy to achieve, it's not. It takes time to learn how to simply be with it, to want to feel compassion for yourself, and then to let it reside within you.

When you're ready, take a deep breath and exhale it as slowly and completely as you can. Then, taking up your pen, write down descriptions of the sensations that parts of your body experience when different feelings course through you. Write your descriptions on the next page.

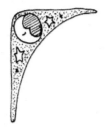
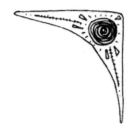

Cultivating Compassion for Your Feelings

*Compassion isn't some kind of self-improvement project or ideal that we're trying to live up to.
Having compassion starts and ends with having compassion for all those unwanted parts of ourselves,
all those imperfections that we don't even want to look at.*

—Pema Chodron

We torture ourselves. We're cruel. Judgmental. We inflict such hate on ourselves. Oh the mind-battles you go through when you try to think yourself *out* of how you feel, when you doubt how you feel, or are challenged by someone about how you feel. It's no surprise, especially if you came from a family that lived by the code that dysfunctional families have lived by for decades: Don't Talk, Don't Think, Don't Feel.

Our daily feelings are mixed with old, "dried paint" feelings—stored feelings from the past—and combined with new and immediate feelings. Those of us who grew up in an environment with rigidity, or the opposite—a complete lack of structure—had little room for being ourselves (that is, lovely and imperfect). And so it's no surprise if we struggle with demonstrating unbridled compassion toward ourselves.

Remember your inner child? Picture your small body and face. Regard that being with love, and appreciate its innocence and grace. Encourage that child—You—with hope. Honor that child with belief. Respect that child by allowing him or her to have, and feel, all imaginable feelings—without judgment, and without fixing. Breathe in, fill your lungs, then exhale all of it with a *whooooo* sound. Feel that relief. That is the relief of letting go of what you *should* feel, and feeling what you actually *do* feel.

Think of a few situations and moments from your daily life. Then examine what your accompanying inner dialogue looks like in terms of three aspects: the situation, your feelings, and how you judge or suppress those feelings.

SITUATION: First, write down the situation or what is happening when you have a feeling and then react to that feeling (say you spilled coffee, forgot a meeting, or got lost driving somewhere).

FEELINGS: Next, write down the accompanying feeling(s) you had, as many as occurred (embarrassed for spilling, disoriented about forgetting, or powerless for getting lost).

JUDGE AND SUPPRESSOR: Last, write down what the "feelings police" in your mind say to convince you that you don't feel what you feel, shouldn't feel what you feel, or need to stop feeling.

You may feel stiff about this at first, and it may seem like very little is coming to mind, but keep on with the activity because your brain will warm up and ideas will come. (And just a reminder: You don't have to be perfect at any activity in this book.)

A couple of examples:

SITUATION: *I am at work, and I'm looking at email rather than answering any, re-marking what I read as "unread."*

FEELINGS: *I'm feeling totally overwhelmed, overloaded with work, bewildered, and unprepared.*

JUDGE AND SUPPRESSOR: *I just look at email and then do nothing. Wake up! Other people stay on top of email. I've got to buck up, focus, and get to it.*

SITUATION: *coming home, seeing dishes still undone and piled up by the sink.*

FEELINGS: *exhausted, defeated, resentful.*

JUDGE AND SUPPRESSOR: *This kind of stuff doesn't exhaust other people. Of course you feel defeated, you can't even manage the simplest thing. Your life is hanging by a thin thread.*

Whether it was a package that you addressed wrong and brought to the post office, or feelings about a date or a business meeting you're not sure went very well—write it all down and recollect and record the feelings you felt and the thoughts you heaped onto yourself. No matter how small a moment it was or how big of a situation it felt like, write it down.

SITUATION:

FEELINGS:

JUDGE AND SUPPRESSOR:

SITUATION:

FEELINGS:

JUDGE AND SUPPRESSOR:

☆ ☆ ☆ ☆ ☆ ☆ ☆

SITUATION:

FEELINGS:

JUDGE AND SUPPRESSOR:

SITUATION:

FEELINGS:

JUDGE AND SUPPRESSOR:

☆ ☆ ★ ☆ ☆ ☆

Look back at what you wrote—in particular, the Judge and Suppressor. Now, do some additional thoughtful writing and dig a bit deeper.

A few questions you can ask yourself would be:

*   In what way am I hard on myself?

*   How do I compare myself to others?

*   How often do I compare myself to others?

*   What would happen if I reacted to myself with more compassion?

*   What's the benefit of thinking about myself like this?

*   What would I say to someone I deeply respected in my same situation?

*   What's another way?

Write your thoughts on the following page.

When you allow yourself to have your feelings and honor them as valid and
acceptable, you can experience the wave rolling in and then out—the sensation
of having feelings as well as self-respect.

Rather than view your Judge and Suppressor simply and as wholly "bad," use what that big uninvited creep has to say, and encourage it to yield something useful.

Refer to your earlier scenarios, and while regarding yourself from a perspective of compassion, write again about how you felt. This time the goal is to embrace your feelings as valid and troubleshoot a kind way forward.

I FELT: First, make note of the feelings you had as specifically as you can.

THAT'S REALISTIC, ALLOWED, AND OK BECAUSE: Next, acknowledge that you have good reason to make mistakes, forget things, drop things, get tired, and to be human. (I've included the word "because" as a prompt, but honestly, just write whatever you feel is valid and doesn't require justification.)

WHAT I CAN DO IS: Last, make a plan for how to move forward.

For example:

I FELT: *overwhelmed*

THAT'S REALISTIC, ALLOWED, AND OK WITH ME BECAUSE: *this volume of email is overwhelming, and overwhelm is a normal response. And, I do have a full To-Do list as it is. Plus, I like to be careful and thorough and there's not room or time for it in this situation.*

WHAT I CAN DO IS: *schedule three times a day to respond to email, challenge myself to write short responses, answer urgent stuff first, allow myself to make spelling mistakes, and flag the non-urgent stuff a certain color.*

I FELT: *exhausted and defeated*

THAT'S REALISTIC, ALLOWED, AND OK WITH ME BECAUSE: *I had a long day and of course I'm exhausted; it's completely and totally understandable. I'm human!*

WHAT I CAN DO IS: *not do it right away, or take the night off from dishes, or ask for help, or change tack and play ABBA while I tackle the dishes to make it fun.*

The key is to include your feelings and make room for them to exist. That's different from being owned by or ruled by your feelings. This may surprise you, but when you stuff or ignore your feelings, you're actually stoking them, maintaining a low burn, and allowing them to be in control. By acknowledging your feelings—"Hello, Exhaustion" or "Hello, Fear"—you are taking the reins, compassionately and lovingly.

I FELT:

THAT'S REALISTIC, ALLOWED, AND OK BECAUSE:

WHAT I CAN DO IS:

I FELT:

THAT'S REALISTIC, ALLOWED, AND OK BECAUSE:

WHAT I CAN DO IS:

- - - - - - - - - - - - -

I FELT:

THAT'S REALISTIC, ALLOWED, AND OK BECAUSE:

WHAT I CAN DO IS:

It takes faith and courage to invite the weary stranger of Truth into your house in the middle of the night and offer him a meal. Yet it leads to transformation. If you lock up your heart, turn out the lights, and hide, who's really in charge?

BOUTS OF WORTHLESSNESS, FEAR, AND HANDLING YOURSELF WITH COMPASSION

Intuitively, we all know that it's better to feel than not to feel.
Beyond their energizing subjective charge, emotions have crucial survival value. They orient us,
interpret the world for us, and offer us vital information. They tell us what is dangerous and what is
benign, what threatens our existence and what will nurture our growth.

—GABOR MATÉ

As you become more self-aware and grow, the greater number of joyful moments you'll experience. The feelings you will feel will be more diverse—not just good versus bad, but a kaleidoscope of feelings. When you befriend your feelings, you begin to notice more subtle and layered feelings, not just the fuse-blowing stentorian ones. And no feeling is less valid than any other. It's just as important to observe dark moments in your growth as it is to bound and leap about ebullient ones. You can safely observe the darkness when it slides in, because you're bigger than it is.

Having a difficult morning is tough. But is it bad? No, and it is normal. Keeping in mind that mornings can have a life of their own can help keep the perfectionist mind in check when it wants you to freak out because you feel sadness tugging at you, or frustration at the coffee grounds that exploded all over your kitchen floor, or anger that your shirt caught and ripped on a hidden nail. When you decide that it's not okay to be annoyed or frustrated about accidents, you are rejecting your feelings, and that will always backfire—just like with a car. *Boom-pop!* Sparks fly, and anger ignites. Unacknowledged, the raw feeling can trigger a downward free-fall into worthlessness, and we'll hear a voice in our mind that we think is our own, criticizing us, cutting us down: *Rah ha ha ha! Look at you, smug, thinking you're all that and part of the normal, perfect human race. Think again. You're still just you, still the crap you began as. Get real, man. Step off the sidewalk and back into the gutter where you know you'll be more comfortable.*

A free-fall into worthlessness is a truly human experience, and it is an opportunity like no other for kindness cultivation. A bout of worthlessness is like getting sick: it requires tender loving care (even if as a culture we are fond of "toughing it out").

Don't push when you free-fall; instead, comfort and nurse yourself. The struggle will actually be shorter. Worthlessness is a human experience, a state of temporary disorientation and depletion, as if an inner compass malfunctioned, making us feel lost and deeply adrift.

In time this will happen less because your "deep" fabric will become stronger and more tightly woven, its holes patched by doing this work.

Swim with Your Fear

When record-breaking swimmer Diana Nyad was asked if she ever felt afraid of training in large bodies of water in which she could not see land or through the blackness—swimming for as many as ten to twenty hours—her answer was, "Of course." The interviewer was surprised and wanted to know how she dealt with it and conquered her fear. I was surprised by her answer: "I don't. I just swim with it."

That is the definition of courage: swimming with the fear. Rather than uphold "fearlessness" as an admirable trait, why not celebrate the courageous act of living, loving, and trying despite our fears?

You can swim with your fear in life in a variety of athletic and non-athletic ways. Public speaking is one of the most common of all human fears—even among public speakers. Other human fears are enclosed spaces, heights, flying, water (lakes, ocean, swimming pools), trains, bridges, and crowds, and of course spiders, snakes, and mice. More poignant are our fears of abstract outcomes: the unknown, lack of control, disappointing ourselves, failure, and even success. You might fear failure because it's embarrassing and you've yet to cultivate the self-compassion to take failure in stride. You might fear success because you sense that with success—which is to say *experience*—you will be changed by it.

Maybe you fear that you'll give up on your training, or injure yourself, before it's time to run the 10K—yet you will train anyway with your fear alongside you. Perhaps you're feeling too wretched to go to a social event, yet you'll clean yourself up and go, taking your fear along to the party. Maybe you fear being fired, yet you acknowledge the overwhelm and work on your top priorities, fear in tow.

Why not start a project or make plans for new experiences that you can't know the outcomes of? If you're scared, anxious, or worried, consider agreeing to plans or projects with a spontaneous mind frame. While you may not be able to visualize the end result, jump in. Take your fear with you. Here's how an acknowledgement of your fear and supportive pact with yourself might look:

EVEN IF … *I'm afraid I won't like the surgeon they assigned me,*

I COULD *make a list of questions to ask about the procedure, voice my concerns, get all the information I need, and know what my options are.*

EVEN IF … *I'm afraid that this blind date will be yet another dead-end,*

I COULD *enjoy the meal and our time together, and find out what this woman thinks about things that are important to her and just see where things go.*

EVEN IF ... *I fear that my work experience isn't competitive or impressive to employers,*
I COULD STILL *apply to the jobs that seem interesting and that match my skills and goals.*

Keep in mind that chefs, athletes, entrepreneurs, and leaders all struggle with worthlessness, fear, and shame. Paramedics, school teachers, college students, artists, retirees, yoga instructors, healers, newsstand clerks, bus drivers—any grown-up child of alcoholic or addict parents battles this. You are not alone.

EVEN IF . . .

I COULD STILL . . .

EVEN IF . . .

I COULD STILL . . .

EVEN IF . . .

I COULD STILL . . .

EVEN IF . . .

I COULD STILL . . .

When a deep, seemingly unshakable sense of worthlessness strikes, there is an opportunity to engage with it. A few questions to ask of your fear are:

WHO ARE YOU?

Acknowledge that fear—or shame, worry, anxiety, or whatever the more prominent feeling may be for you—has stricken. Say to yourself, "This feeling is happening," then put a label on it. You may say, "I'm feeling fearful," or "This is that worthlessness that adult children of dysfunctional families sometimes grapple with."

TO WHOM DO YOU BELONG?

Remind yourself that your shame and identification with being worthless is an inheritance —it's not the true you. The fear or shame has its roots in the long line of scared survivalists who were too immature to raise you and your kin with emotional intelligence.

WHY DON'T YOU SIT OVER THERE?

You can use your imagination to separate who you are and what your fear is. Try to imagine your fear as something coming from outside you that's attempting to imbed itself, as opposed to something within you. Use some imagery to distance yourself from it, like seeing your fear as exhaust wafting toward you from a passing bus that you hold your breath to avoid inhaling. Use imagery to see your fear as a balloon or bubble floating that you can physically blow away with a puff of breath.

FEAR, WHY DID YOU COME?

Once you have observed your fear, you can investigate it. Since it's there, you may as well ask it *why*. "Why this visit?" or "What triggered your arrival?" or "Might you be here to distract me? Are you here to steer me away from doing something I might be afraid to do yet later proud of?"

Are you afraid to be great? Do you fear unleashing your power, opinion, questions, and dreams? Is it possible you're waiting for permission to be yourself or to express and discover your talents? I know it can be a long wait. I waited for validation of my beliefs for decades, along with validation of my suspicions about my talents and gifts. I thought I might have something to share with the world, but I waited for someone of esteem to tell me I was right. I also waited a long time for people to lift me up and agree with me about the smart things to do with my life. One day, I became aware that I was holding out for approval—and stopped waiting. I decided I could do the job of living and simply believe in myself. When that validation and agreement about being right came, at last, from within me, it resonated deeply.

Surviving a tough childhood required rejecting our needs, being unseen, and also being very cautious. As a result, we may not be sure as adults that we are supposed to have good things happen to us. We may not be entirely convinced that we are worth happiness or deserve good things, which tends to make us hesitant. Yet, the fact that fear exists doesn't mean you have to wait to live your life. There is no reason you can't take your fear with you; let it travel alongside you by slinging it over your shoulder, holding its hand, or snapping it on like an unsightly fanny pack. "Who's that?" others might ask. "Oh, that's my fear," you'll say. "He didn't want me to come tonight, so I had to take him along."

I'm in Love with Your Anger!

Bitterness is like cancer. It eats upon the host. But anger is like fire. It burns it all clean.
—Maya Angelou

Anger, I see you. Tell me your story, and I will listen. I am not afraid of you.

We give anger its explosive power the moment we attempt to repress or ignore it. When we acknowledge the anger, that is actually the first step to diffusing and transforming it. We notice anger, yet it is not the first emotion to arrive; it's often second to the party, impairing the first. Anger is, frequently, the result of our attempt to squelch feelings of hurt, embarrassment, or shame. A simple, universal example is the experience of physical hurt. A hammer comes down on your thumb while you're trying to pound a nail into the wall. Bam! Ouch! You react with anger, throwing down the hammer or stamping your foot. Ow! Damn hammer! Damn nail! Damn me!

Hurt sometimes transforms into anger lightning-fast, while other times it can evolve from a slow burn of unvoiced resentment over time. Say you're waiting for your brother or old friend to show up for lunch, but they're late. They text to let you know, but they are later than the text said they'd be. And by the time they arrive, you're mad. This is not the first time.

When anger strikes, the question to ask is, "What do I need to do or say in this situation?" The second question to ask is, "Can I say or do that with compassion?" For example, you may say to yourself: "Do I need to stop waiting for my brother or friend, just head back home, and try meeting for lunch again another time? Do I need to use the time to go run an errand or call a friend? Can I keep waiting, but let them know that it wasn't fun to wait?" Then you may say to the person when he arrives: "I have a lot going on today, and I would rather have rescheduled than waited. Could you let me know next time you're running that late?" (As opposed to, "You're always late—what's up with that?!")

If you're not going to mute, swallow, or numb your feelings with eating, spending, or checking out in some other fashion, then what's left? The feelings must be felt. The only way to navigate feelings is to feel them, to let them roll up and over you like a wave (and wave to it as it passes on by).

HAVE A WITNESS

Having a *witness* to your anger and experiences is therapeutic, and I believe it's essential to the passage. A witness is someone who will listen and not be overwhelmed by what you have to share, and who can reflect back for you what you're feeling. For example, "That must have been extremely painful," or "You must have felt deeply betrayed." There are many different types of witnesses with whom you can share strong, angry, painful feelings: a therapist, a priest, a twelve-step group, group therapy, or a trusted friend. A witness doesn't tell you what to do or try to minimize your experience. That's why the process is so powerful and validating when it goes well. Being listened to with compassion is a gift.

EN MEDIA RES

This work is done in the middle of things. If only we could stop the vehicle of our lives to do this work. If only we could take a huge break from it all in order to do the work of fixing ourselves, and continue on only when we're ready. And yet, working on ourselves in the middle of our lives gives us immediate opportunities to put new tools to work.

Therapeutic group settings are effective for healing because you get to hear the stories of so many others like you, in addition to sharing your own. This transforms your own story, allowing it to be witnessed and released, and then helps you neutralize the shame about it when you see just how normal it is. The best part is that you see you're not alone. As you share and share again, the powerful memories and feelings begin to have less power over you.

I'm in Love with Your Anger!

One of my favorite films is *In America*. It contains a scene about anger that is a turning point for the main character (Johnny). In this scene, Johnny, who is numbed of all feeling following the death of his son, confronts the handsome and mysterious artist next door (Mateo) who has been spending more and more time with Johnny's wife and daughters.

```
                        Johnny
              Are you in love with her?

                        Mateo
    No. I'm in love with you. And I'm in love with your beautiful
    woman. And I'm in love with your kids. And I'm even in love with
    your unborn child. I'm even in love with your anger! I'm in love
                   with anything that lives!
```

Mateo is *even in love with Johnny's anger*. He is in love with all embodiments of life, which includes feelings as proof of living, of being alive. To feel is to live. Anger is merely a feeling—a real-deal, living and breathing feeling.

Anger gets a bad rap in our culture, but it's not anger itself that's bad. It's a natural feeling that occurs in humans, so it can't be "wrong." The negative reputation of anger comes from its being badly expressed, and our association of anger with frenzy—violent actions, chairs hurled, punches thrown, or yelling at strangers. We don't tend to see *good* examples of anger; rarely do we witness it as a feeling that comes, rolls through, and then dissipates and transforms like any other. Our parents likely did not model for us how to process anger, and they very likely ignored or criticized our anger, so that renders us pretty unprepared for transforming anger in adulthood. We're lacking that lesson, yet when we get it, we realize that anger can teach us about ourselves.

When anger rises in me, it stems from some form of hurt. Anger is a second feeling, not the foremost, root feeling. Our feelings get hurt, then we get MAD. Gosh, it happens fast! We react from the anger rather than from the truth of the hurt, so we say, "That bastard didn't call me back. What a jerk!" When, really what we feel under it all is, "I noticed that we didn't talk today. I really wanted to hear his voice." (There's information at hand: this must mean I like him!) Because we value strength and control over vulnerability in our culture, we enact our anger rather than our hurt. We say, "Why didn't you call?!" and the communication gets off on the wrong foot. We don't say the truth—"I missed hearing your voice yesterday"—because we fear states of vulnerability and we buy into the code of staying in control. Physical hurt, too, can turn into an angry response. Say you stub your toe and rather than coddle yourself, you shout, "Damn it!" at the chair that has always been in the same spot. As humans, we bump into things. We are clumsy sometimes. And we are also beautiful. We are imperfect.

Imagine being around someone you trust to feel angry feelings and then to handle their anger—someone who owns it and doesn't point it toward you or anyone else. How does it feel to imagine that experience? Now imagine being able to handle your own anger. Imagine knowing what anger feels like in your being, to recognize it and not be afraid of it. Imagine yourself feeling it, unafraid, and wanting to know why it's there and what it has to tell you. What is it like to imagine that anger and fear?

Acknowledging your anger compassionately is an act of validating it. It's also a healing act. To acknowledge a feeling of anger, first notice the sensations it causes inside you and identify the source of it. What incident triggered it? Try to identify the source in a blameless way, such as, "I'm angry that they wrote the check for the wrong amount," rather than, "I'm angry because they're trying to cheat me of my pay."

Then, once you've named your anger and its source, reflect back to yourself that your reaction is *okay*. By doing this you are sending a powerful message to yourself—and to that child deep inside you—that your feelings are okay. You are learning to accept and comfort yourself from the inside-out.

WHAT DO YOU THINK ABOUT ANGER?

You have a right to feel your feelings, whatever they are. And while anger can be one of the more difficult ones to feel and to accept, it is a feeling no different from excitement and fatigue. They are fluid; they come to you, rising and falling and ebbing and flowing like waves on the sea.

The tricky part is this: when you grow up in a dysfunctional, codependent, or chaotic childhood home, you tend to get pulled into the wave of anger and let it take you, envelop you, and drag you out to sea, rather than being empowered to resist it and to be anchored. And when we can't withstand the feeling and let it roll over us, we instead go inactive, numb, or *disassociate*. Other times we react in a big, huge, fiery way, rather than in proportion to the situation, our needs, or our wants.

Anger in particular may sometimes feel bigger and more powerful than you are.

It's not.

When you can acknowledge anger and say, "Hello, Anger," that will tip the scales and remind you that you're in charge. You can then, from an anchored position, begin to ask questions of your anger: Why did this anger come? Does it make you feel uneasy? Why? What's the worst thing that could happen if you *feel* this anger?

Take some time to do an inventory of your thoughts, feelings, and assumptions about anger.

Every human feels anger. Depending upon the culture in which you grew up, the expression of anger may have been unacceptable in your home. It's also possible that when you witnessed anger growing up, it went unexplained and was even treated as if it didn't happen.

You've had some practice with identifying how feelings feel in your body, both emotionally and physically, and the reactions you have to them, which will be useful as you focus on *anger* specifically. Below, write about what you can observe about how anger feels for you. Start by recalling a recent situation that angered you. Bring it to life by closing your eyes and picturing the situation, the people, and the place involved with you in the scene. Then write down what you can observe of your anger.

Bodily sensations I notice when feelings of anger arise in me:

My judgments about anger are:

What I fear with regard to my anger:

The role of anger (theirs, my own) while growing up was:

GETTING IT ALL OUT

This is a rare invitation for you to be honest about what has angered you. Get it *all* out! If you're not sure if the feeling is red-hot anger or, say, red-hot frustration, go ahead and include both grades of feelings here.

☆ ⭐ ☆ ☆ ⭐ ⭐

You can write *I feel angry* rather than *I am* angry to help remind yourself that you're *feeling* something as opposed to *being* something.

Your parents may not have taught you the important difference between disappointing actions and a disappointing person. (What was modeled for me was: disappointing actions throw a person's character and worth into question, all or nothing, with no gray area.) You have permission to feel angry about anything. Don't concern yourself about whether things you've been angry about are things that "shouldn't" bother you.

Shouldn't? Says *who*?

Throw those "shoulds" out the window; they will come up but toss them. "Should" and feelings don't mix—they are opposites like oil and water (if not enemies).

For example, I might write: I feel angry *that my parents didn't regard me as smart and feed my curiosity and intellect. I was always in awe of smart people yet never knew I was one.*

What do you have to say about anger? Use this page to write about things that have angered you.

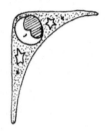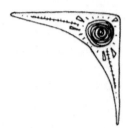

CONVERSING (WITH CURIOSITY) WITH YOUR ANGER

You are learning the art of slowing down enough to stop and *see* your anger and to converse compassionately with it. Anger is normal, human, and a useful tool for learning about your wants and needs (yeah, those things we too often push aside).

Now, refer to the anger you wrote about on the previous page and compassionately acknowledge the validity of your angry feelings. This is a form of healing *self-parenting*—you can and should use and reuse this technique on yourself (as well as extend it to those you care about).

AN EXAMPLE: a grown man is angry that his parents didn't acknowledge or nurture his intellect:

You have every right to feel angry that your parents didn't see your intelligence and talents and didn't help you cultivate them. You deserved more. I would feel angry feelings, too. Just so you know, I am okay with your feeling angry, okay? You're allowed to feel anger. It's a part of life, and it doesn't define you or envelop you. And if you have trouble managing your anger, we'll get help and deal with that. So, see? There's nothing that we can't handle!

I'm angry that:

Words of compassion for my anger as my own loving parent:

I'm angry that:

Words of compassion for my anger as my own loving parent:

I'm angry that:

Words of compassion for my anger as my own loving parent:

The unconscious is shy, elusive, and unwieldy,

but it is possible to learn to tap it at will, and even to direct it.

The conscious mind is meddlesome, opinionated, and arrogant,

but it can be made subservient to the inborn talent through training.

By isolating as far as possible the functions of these two sides of the mind,

even by considering them not merely as aspects of the same mind but as separate

personalities, we can arrive at a kind of working metaphor,

impossible to confuse with reality, but infinitely helpful in self-eduction.

—DOROTHEA BRANDE, "BECOMING A WRITER"

PART THREE:
Navigating
SABOTAGE

ON SELF-SABOTAGE

You can silence the Saboteur with acts of courage and by following your intuition. It serves you brilliantly as a gut instinct that directs you to take action based on hunches rather than on rational thought. To learn to experience that voice, you must respond to it. Only through response can you manifest the courage to expand your creating environment. Start with small choices, which may be life-transforming acts of will disguised as harmless impulses.

—CAROLYN MYSS

Self-sabotage is a term that can evoke shame and is used too often against ourselves. It is also an inaccurate way to describe what is going on when we fail to complete a task, leave a project unfinished, or can't seem to reach our goals. We toss around the term sabotage quite casually: You were late for your appointment? Self-sabotage! You're getting laid off from your job? Self-sabotage! You didn't call your girlfriend when you said you would? You're sabotaging your relationship! You sabotaged my party! You sabotaged our marriage! And on, and on.

Yet does self-sabotage actually exist?

Consider these definitions: *sabotage* is a plot to undermine an outcome, either intentional or not, while *self-sabotage* is a plot against our own intentions and one that is *un*intentional.

That self-sabotage is unintentional makes it all the more sinister. When we use the term self-sabotage, we accuse ourselves of a hidden desire to fail, of holding an intent to derail our own efforts. And so self-sabotage becomes a demon of our own making, one we summon and scare and shame ourselves with. We are victims of the myth of self-sabotage, and when we believe the myth—that we are being capsized by our unconscious, by an inner, secret desire to fail—we are propagating it and create for ourselves an endless cycle. As a result, we cede power when we should not, and we forego it when, actually, we indeed possess the power to reach our goals.

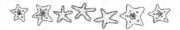

What we call "self-sabotage" is actually one or both of these realities happening: disinterest or lack of planning.

That's it. Not terribly dramatic or exciting, but true. Self-sabotage is simply a side effect of our lack of experience with good planning, and inexperience with what it takes to finish things. We also sometimes take on projects that we're not truly interested in.

If you were raised in a dysfunctional family, you might not have much experience with completing projects easily. It is unlikely that your parents took the time to help you learn how to break down a larger project into tasks with a timeline, making the project manageable and easy to complete. If you have a large project on your plate and you're not sure how to plan each part of it so that you're sure to complete it, you will become overwhelmed, are highly likely to procrastinate, and are sure to be working all-out in the final hour or past the deadline.

Self-sabotage also stems from not making decisions at all, allowing the passage of time to steer the results, and for the decisions to be made for us. Deadlines will come and go if you do nothing. If you want to apply to graduate school, for example, and do nothing to make that happen, you may regard what happened as "self-sabotage" rather than poor planning. Next comes the sense of defeat along with dread and lying. We often lie to ourselves, saying that we wanted to do the project we failed to start or finish, when perhaps we weren't aware that the project simply wasn't interesting. There is likewise a sense of hiding or invisibility that accompanies self-sabotage. For example, I may keep to myself that I'm disappointed, that the project was important, that I was "going for it" but missed the boat, or that I have a hope, a dream, ideas. And then, as always, there arises the feeling of shame about it all, and that is when we mutter or think the horrible term "self-sabotage."

DISINTEREST OR LACK OF PLANNING MASQUERADES AS SELF-SABOTAGE

Bring to mind a few relationships, commitments, jobs, projects, or physical training goals you have attempted but didn't finish or resolve for which you suspect self-sabotage was in play. Write them down, consider them, and then think about to what degree poor planning played a role and what level of interest you had.

SITUATION:

HOW INTERESTED IN THE OUTCOME AND THE PROCESS WAS I?

DID I CONSIDER DETAILS AND STEPS, AND CAREFULLY SCHEDULE THEM?

SITUATION:

HOW INTERESTED IN THE OUTCOME AND THE PROCESS WAS I?

DID I CONSIDER DETAILS AND STEPS, AND CAREFULLY SCHEDULE THEM?

SITUATION:

HOW INTERESTED IN THE OUTCOME AND THE PROCESS WAS I?

DID I CONSIDER DETAILS AND STEPS, AND CAREFULLY SCHEDULE THEM?

SITUATION:

HOW INTERESTED IN THE OUTCOME AND THE PROCESS WAS I?

DID I CONSIDER DETAILS AND STEPS, AND CAREFULLY SCHEDULE THEM?

Time is a fascinating creature. It is definite, concrete, and inflexible on one hand, while on the other it can seem a bit elastic, depending on our level of expertise and confidence.

Consider the projects you just wrote about. Now, through writing, investigate the projects further and examine why they're incomplete. Ask yourself a couple of tough questions:

* Am I able to complete this now?
* Do I need to take a break from it and push a different project forward?

When you abandon or delay a project through an informed decision to do so, you are initiating an action full of courage and wisdom. But if you've come to a standstill, you perhaps merely need to identify the next small step.

Consider two or three of the following additional questions and investigate them with further writing:

* What inspired the endeavor?

* Who was the outcome for?

* Why was I doing it?

* Did I really choose it, or did I fall into it?

* What did I want to get from the project?

* Is the relationship important to me?

* Is the job important to me?

* Did I just want out and go about it in a cowardly way?

* Did an issue come up?

* Was I avoiding conflict?

* Did I know what the next three steps were?

* Why was I interested in the project?

When do your answers come quickly? What questions are you not ready to ask of yourself? Are there questions you're altogether avoiding? Why is that? Notice your avoidance as it holds big clues.

THE WILD MIND

The addict seldom questions the reality of the unpleasant mood or feeling she wants to escape.
She rarely examines the perspective from which her mind experiences and understands the world
around her and from which she hears and sees people in her life. She is in a constant state of
reactivity—not to the world so much as to her own interpretations of it.
The distressing internal state is not examined; the focus is entirely on the outside:
What can I receive from the world that will make me feel okay, if only for a moment?

—GABOR MATÉ

We have such imaginations! They can create wonderful buildings, art, movies, and technology. We humans have always been able to imagine other worlds and create stories about them, yet we're suckers for imagined criticism, judgment, and rejection, believing all of it! Our wild minds are extremely convincing.

Everyone doubts themselves; it is an unavoidable aspect of the human mind. But while each of us doubts ourselves, we each react differently to it. Some of us take the doubting voices in our head seriously, as if they were voicing legitimate concerns or even warnings. Some of us battle the voices and get slowed down by them. Still others of us notice the voices, yet swat them away like the momentary, buzzing distractions they usually are and stay the course.

The mind is wild, but you hold the reins.

Learning to love ourselves and feel compassionately toward ourselves requires that we take time to think about what we truly believe. What do you think, independent of others' opinions? Do you say what you think, or do you "bookend" what you say by adding a type of apology, loophole, contradiction, or joke to what you've just said or are about to say? When our self-esteem is weak, it can feel too risky to express ourselves honestly because we are defending against anxieties about setting off an angry person or offending someone, or we're attempting to manipulate the reactions of others or avoid situations in which we have to defend or explain our truest opinions and selves.

The act of feeling compassion for our personal truth—whatever it may be—is also an act of getting to know ourselves. The two occur in concert. It's not our fault if we are living according to a code that doesn't quite fit, one that we're unsure how to shake off or tweak. Children adopt the beliefs and attitudes of the people who raised them, and in the best-case scenarios, that process supports our species and society. When the scenario is less than ideal, we grow up confused about our needs and are distracted by a nagging feeling that we don't quite fit in like others in society.

Probing the Wild Mind

We tend to repeat patterns that we don't bother to evaluate, probe, or test. It takes practice to identify the distinction between a critical voice in your mind that's actually your own and a critical, blaming voice whose origins are your mother, father, grandparent, or siblings —or even an old boss, former friend, coach, etc. When the voice in your head is critical to the point of self-loathing, that voice's origins aren't you. As such, it's helpful to separate their voices from yours so that you can begin to stop taking ownership of criticisms that aren't yours and to ferret out criticisms that you don't actually agree with. Once you find out who's in your head, you know who you're dealing with—and disagreeing with. You might be surprised to find your father-in-law's voice—or his imagined judgments— showing up more often than your father's.

Consider the past week or two, starting with today. Was there a moment in which you can remember thinking harshly, critically, or devoid of compassion toward yourself during a task, project, or interaction?

An example:

EVENT: *Missed an 8 a.m. phone meeting*

WILD MIND/CRITICISM: *"High-achievers check the next day's agenda before bed."*

WHOSE VOICE/SOURCE: *An ex-boss*

ACCUSATION/VALUE ATTACK: *Dreamers aren't achievers; they're spacey and self-centered.*

TRUE BELIEF: *It happens. Everyone misses meetings sometimes. I rarely plan early-morning meetings and shouldn't set them up if I can avoid it. When I need to, though, I have to set up a reminder.*

Or:

EVENT: *Still unemployed*

WILD MIND/CRITICISM: *"Even Jax got a job and he never went to college."*

WHOSE VOICE/SOURCE: *Aunt*

ACCUSATION/VALUE ATTACK: *You're a lone wolf; only the best will do; you're selfish.*

TRUE BELIEF: *I could get any old job, but I have a plan and believe in it, even if others don't get it.*

When we can stop ripping ourselves to shreds in our minds and treat ourselves with the kindness and compassion we have a right to, we then know how to extend that kindness and acceptance to those we love deeply: our mates, families, and children.

What critical summations have you netted yourself with? Draw them out of the depths, and write them down on the next page.

EVENT:

WILD MIND/CRITICISM:

WHOSE VOICE/SOURCE:

ACCUSATION/VALUE ATTACK:

TRUE BELIEF:

☆ ✹ ☆ ☆ ☆ ✦ ☆

EVENT:

WILD MIND/CRITICISM:

WHOSE VOICE/SOURCE:

ACCUSATION/VALUE ATTACK:

TRUE BELIEF:

☆ ✹ ☆ ☆ ☆ ✦ ☆

EVENT:

WILD MIND/CRITICISM:

WHOSE VOICE/SOURCE:

ACCUSATION/VALUE ATTACK:

TRUE BELIEF:

EVENT:

WILD MIND/CRITICISM:

WHOSE VOICE/SOURCE:

ACCUSATION/VALUE ATTACK:

TRUE BELIEF:

DECIDING WHAT IT IS THAT YOU WANT

Growing up in a dysfunctional home trains us to detect and prioritize the feelings and needs of others before our own. With enough practice at determining the needs of others, and knowing that fulfilling those needs restores calm to the household, we lose the ability to tune in to our own feelings and needs. Over time we become people who truly aren't sure what we want. This makes what seems like simple decision-making (to outsiders) difficult and sometimes impossible. But if, like me, you've been asked, "What do you mean you don't know what movie you'd prefer to see?" you understand what it's like to simply not know.

There are certainly times that a decision isn't necessary, and in some cases time itself resolves things. There are times when making a decision isn't critical, or when you need to focus on a goal larger than a particular decision. Yet when you do make decisions, whether large or small, the process you use will help to regenerate and strengthen the connections between your true needs and wants and your feelings.

Try this new twist on the classic pro-and-con decision-making list. It can be used for decisions as simple as where to go for dinner or choosing what shirt or shoes to wear to an event, as well as bigger decisions like whether or not to sell or buy a car, or whether to go back to school.

Begin by dividing a sheet of paper into four sections and drawing a cross that fills the page. This will give you four spaces in which you can note pros and cons, as well as the corresponding feelings you have about them. For example:

PRACTICAL PRO

Masters degrees are good to have, no matter what the subject is

It would help me get a teaching job

I'll learn to write better more quickly, and that saves time

PRACTICAL CON

I would have to take loans and be in debt

Takes money I don't have

An MFA degree doesn't make me more employable

Very hard to work full-time and do school too

Sacrifice of two years

I don't "need" an MFA—it's "nice to have" and costly

I'll believe in myself more if I have a higher degree

I'll think of myself as a writer, and others are more likely to as well

Self-esteem boost

An act of self-care and love of myself

Can't be called "dumb"

It'll save me from turning into my alcoholic mother

My dad will be proud of me

I'm too old at this point

People think creative writing degrees are a joke

Getting asked if I'm working on the Great American Novel feels like being shamed

Who do I think I am?!

My stepmom will think I'm trying to out-educate her

I'd be getting a second useless degree

FEELINGS PRO

FEELINGS CON

Use this space for your own decision-making that includes both pros and cons, and your feelings too.

PRACTICAL PRO   PRACTICAL CON

FEELINGS PRO   FEELINGS CON

Once you've completed the grid, note your insights on the next page.

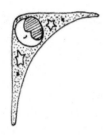

Sinking Self-Sabotage

Spectacular achievement is preceded by unspectacular preparation.
—Robert H. Schuller

Success, to the soul, means leaving home—"home" being this present moment, your point of view or a familiar routine. Any act of bravery requires a departure from what is already known; abandoning the present and embracing the unknown are ingredients of any definition of "success," and success entails change—of a job, point of view, location, or even a change in you.

There is a relationship between self-sabotage and fear of success. The truth is, self-sabotage is our way of avoiding success. We must ask ourselves: Which is scarier—not succeeding or succeeding? Does the thought of success scare you more than the thought of remaining idle? Does failure seem more comfortable? If so, it's because self-sabotage keeps you right where you are—frustrated, sure, but comfortable.

Change involves a departure, even if small—a departure from yourself as you know yourself, from your body as you know it, from a city or house, or from a group. Yet change is nothing new. It is a constant occurrence in our universe and the reason for our existence. Change happens, in small ways every day of our lives: a new face at the coffee counter; your hot chocolate tastes different; the road is closed and there's a detour; a new coworker, corporate email policy, or dent in your fender; public pay phones have disappeared; they've changed your shampoo formula; gasoline rates have gone up; you get your hair cut; you're a pound lighter, heavier, etc. We are uneasy with change and yet we're in the midst of it on a continual basis.

A difficult but essential question to ask yourself when you suspect that you are sabotaging yourself is whether a part of you feels safer about failing than succeeding. Is it possible that failing to complete a project or engaging in sabotage-laden entanglements serves a purpose? What do you avoid having to face, look at, do, or overcome as long as you hold back and stick to your existing way of living? Does failing keep you "safe?" Whatever you do, or don't do, have the courage to ask those questions.

A Big Idea and One Hundred Small Unseen Steps

We start projects because we are human and driven to create things; we jump into action because we are motivated to do so by our natures. The only difference between someone who leaps into action and the person who finishes projects is this: planning.

When you worry that you are procrastinating or are wondering if you are engaged in self-sabotage, that is the time to ask yourself a question: "Do I know what my next step is?" It is entirely more likely that you haven't yet identified your next step, or don't yet know how to approach it, than you're actually sabotaging yourself.

What if your dream is to make a documentary film? That is a big idea that will probably require a list of steps if you're going to tackle it. (Not all of your projects or ideas will demand such a long or detailed list.)

If you start with a list of ten items like the one on the following page, you've made a good start because this list gives you a sense of the scope of the project and how long it might take.

1. Create script and treatment for film

2. Get funding

3. Assemble crew

4. Plan timeline for whole production

5. Recruit subjects to interview

6. Schedule interviews

7. Conduct interviews and travel

8. Post-production

9. Promotion and marketing

10. Release

The issue is how does one "create a script," "get funding," or "recruit subjects"? The truth is that there are one hundred small, unseen steps that lead to each of the ten items on the list.

For instance, let's take the second step, "get funding," and make a list of steps that lead to that goal.

2. GET FUNDING

(a)   Schedule time to research grants.

(b)   Choose the most appropriate grant.

(c)   Print out application information.

(d)   Carefully read and make notes on the application.

(e)   Schedule time in calendar to think about what to write on the application.

(f)   Evaluate what work examples to include.

(g)   Choose the samples, and refine them if needed.

(h)   Get feedback from someone.

(i)   Schedule time to complete online application and print it out.

(j)   Proofread the application.

(k)   Double-check the rules and guidelines.

(l)   Send the packet.

(m)   Mark the decision date on a calendar for getting the grant funds.

The key is to create sub-lists for your list of ten steps, and even sub-sub-steps as well, when that is helpful. Once you have the sub-steps in mind, you can begin to evaluate how much time you will need to accomplish each of the ten main steps.

How long do you think it might take to make a documentary? A few months? A year? The answer usually is, "longer than you'd think." How long things take is tough to get right with a causal estimate because there is a conflict between real time—how long things actually take, and wishful time—how long we wish things would take.

Here is an example of what a realistic plan might look like:

1. Create script and treatment for film	6 months
2. Get funding	4 months
3. Assemble crew	2 months
4. Plan timeline for whole production	2-3 weekends
5. Recruit subjects to interview	3-5 weeks
6. Schedule interviews	1-2 weeks
7. Conduct interviews and travel	3 months
8. Post-production	2 months
9. Promotion and marketing	4 months
10. Release	22 months from start

If you add up the time that each task may take, you'll see that you're looking at something very close to a two-year project. If you wanted to make a documentary and started this project without writing down the steps involved and without time estimates for each, it's probable that after working on your project for a few months, you would start to feel defeated, as if "nothing is happening." But if you had a list of steps and an under-standing of how long things actually take, you could reassure yourself that you're actually on the right track.

HAVE MAP, HAVE COMPASS, WILL TRAVEL

If you're the kind of person who tends to be hard on yourself, you may find that planning for small tasks and goals feels good and fosters a lot of self-compassion. Think about it: any recipe in a cookbook that says "takes 40 minutes" will likely take at least 90 minutes when you are cooking it for the first time. Likewise, when you are embarking on a project, parti-cularly if it's a first of its kind, you would be wise to double your time, if only to manage your expectations.

Even packing a lunch is an opportunity to plan, to iterate, and to be open-minded. If you have tried to bring your lunch but often forget, try making your lunch before bed, or bringing bread and sandwich ingredients to work and making it there, or making and freezing a few lunches on the weekend, or planning to wake up a half hour early in the morning to prepare a fresh lunch. Write it down. Plan. Trying another way will allow you to find one that works.

Here's another scenario: Have you ever asked yourself in fall or winter how you "forgot" to go on a vacation that year? Did you forget to plan one, or were you so overwhelmed by what it would take to plan and budget for one that you simply avoided it? If so, consider a second type of planning that breaks a vacation down into steps.

Step #1 – Brainstorm and identify the inspiration for the vacation.

* relaxation
* helping/volunteering
* adventure
* education

Step #2 – Identify three options that satisfy this goal.

- ✸ staying in a cabin by a lake for a week
- ✸ building a community center in an impoverished region
- ✸ visiting museums and historical sites

Step #3 – Research the costs involved and timing.

- ✸ identify dates and mark in calendar
- ✸ price out flights, gas, lodging, meals, and entertainment
- ✸ compare in-season (summer) versus off-season costs (fall)
- ✸ compare costs of groceries for a cabin versus meals out in a city
- ✸ identify cost alternatives (house swapping instead of hotel, camping, etc.)

Step #4 – Choose one and plan details.

- ✸ cabin by a lake for a week
- ✸ brainstorm any final details regarding costs, logistics, or timing
- ✸ create a to-do list for the trip

Step #5 – Do it!

- ✸ look forward to your trip
- ✸ tell friends you're going on vacation
- ✸ relax and enjoy yourself!

Aside from paper and pen, which I personally favor—especially long rolls of paper—there are tools like Pinterest available for trolling for ideas and collecting your own, as well as apps such as Things or Workflowy for project management.

Now, on the following page, try a bit of planning yourself.

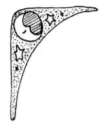

We travel for romance, we travel for architecture, and we travel to be lost.

—Ray Bradbury

VISUALIZE THE SHORELINE

Visualization is a powerful tool. Athletes, for an example, use visualization as a key part of their training, readiness, and success. You have already cultivated your ability to use visualization in order to connect with your inner child and to identify your feelings, and now you can use it to steer yourself toward your goals. As with many powers, the power of visualization has a dark side: used for negative intent, visualization can wreak havoc; it can also change your breathing, create a sick stomach, increase your heart rate, give you chest pains, or cause dizziness—all from the power of imagining worst-case scenarios, betrayal, or catastrophe. Yet harnessed for good, visualization can have equally powerful and positive physiological results.

Visualizing yourself in the act of doing what you hope to do, accomplishing a goal, or facing challenges head-on will soothe your system, right your mind, and strengthen your relationship with your instincts.

With your eyes either open or closed and sitting comfortably, try this visualization:

Picture yourself as you approach your goal. Where is it taking place—in a workshop, in a car, at a desk, on stage, in a grassy field? What are the surroundings? How do you feel? Walk through the motions of what you are about to do. Imagine how your face, mouth, and eyes feel. Consider your feet in their shoes and how they make contact with the ground; picture your hands and what they are grasping. What does the environment around you look like as you visualize yourself? What are you saying? What are you thinking? *See* it as you want it to go.

Now, on the following page, describe what you visualized, in writing.

Big goals are perfect for visualization techniques, but you can also use visualization to turn around the mind's habit of worst-case-scenario thinking as a daily self-healing tool.

A few everyday opportunities for visualization are:

* Visualizing yourself as you arrive early to an appointment and reading a book with the ten minutes you have to spare

* Visualizing your mouth and lips as you say the word "no" to plans that are not realistic for you

* Visualizing the course of your day and, in particular, yourself as you move through the transition moments of your day between tasks and locations

* Visualizing yourself relaxed and content

* Visualizing yourself making a list and prioritizing the items on it, and then starting to work on the first one

* Visualizing yourself asking someone how their day is going

* Visualizing yourself kindly

TIME WARPING

To achieve great things, two things are needed: a plan, and not quite enough time.

—LEONARD BERNSTEIN

We're at war with time. We're resentful about how long things take to start, to arrive, and to get done; we fret about how time seems to runs out. When we think about the word "time," we think *hurry*, we think *deadlines*, and we also think of the only word we fear more than self-sabotage: *procrastination*.

But not only is it fundamentally human to procrastinate, animals do it too—just as you might choose to eat the cake now and work off the weight later, pigeons will choose to eat something that doesn't involve much work, even if it means they'll have to work much harder for the same amount of food later. Consider procrastination the act of prioritizing tasks in a seemingly irrational order, which, when carried out, elicits dread and shame yet can also yield better long-term results.

If you remove the blame and shame from procrastination, it simply becomes a form of prioritization.

In his book *Wait: The Art and Science of Delay*, writer Frank Partnoy retells a great true story about procrastination: George Akerlof was supposed to ship a box from India to the United States for a friend, but he put off doing it. He had the box, which contained his friend's clothes and mementos, for *eight months* before he eventually shipped it to him. Both guilt and shame mounted—"each morning for over eight months I woke up and decided that the *next* morning would be the day to send the Stiglitz box," he wrote in an essay about the ordeal titled, "Procrastination and Obedience" for *American Economic Review* in 1991. I share this story because Akerlof later understood his procrastination as a prioritization issue (he knew that his friend didn't need the items in the box urgently), as well as overwhelm about not knowing how the postal system in India worked. I also share the story because Akerlof isn't "lazy" (the thing we call ourselves when we procrastinate); he's a professor at UC Berkeley and a Nobel-winning economist. His story is a reminder that to procrastinate is to be human.

One way to end our war with time is to stop fighting it. We can't fight a war if we lay down our weapons, right? Is it a war if we admit that twenty-four hours exist in a day, that we must sleep for eight of those, and work for at least eight more? Is it a war if we admit that our commute, conversations, or double-checking our work all takes the time it takes ... if we decide to learn about the other side, understand it, and get some perspective on our reasons for fighting it? We end the time war through understanding and compassion for the "enemy." This means a willingness to see time as it really is and our day-to-day activities as they really are too.

RESENTING TIME

People who grow up in dysfunctional families tend to have unrealistic expectations of time. As children we didn't have helpful models for budgeting time and we didn't get practice with planning ahead, preparing, or determining how many things can be accomplished in a certain period of time. Our solution has been to try to get everything we *want* to get done in a given period of time. We even evoke our *will* to get things done, as if we could bend time. This leads to a kind of anguish, a sense of self-sabotage time and again. *Why can't I get it all done?* you ask. *Why can't I get places on time? How do other people get everything done?*

Anyone who grew up in a dysfunctional home environment has experienced the many blockades that play into our sense of self-sabotage with regard to time:

* ✱   A need to self-soothe
* ✱   Perfectionism
* ✱   Self-criticism
* ✱   A hard time finishing projects

If you grew up within chaos or "excitement," in which things changed and were always new and different (or differently chaotic), you know perfectionism, self-criticism, and more about starts than finishes. You may use some of your time in reaction to a deep craving for safety, comfort, and sameness. You may require more time than someone else to engage in relaxing activities, as well as extra time to transition between tasks; you may need a walk around the block after work and before dinner, or to sit in your car for a few moments before walking into work. Those moments are valuable and often don't require a lot of time. If you refuse yourself those in-between moments, the need to self-soothe may gobble bigger chunks of time at a later point.

How might you feel about time and your pursuits if you didn't have perfectionism, self-criticism, or a fear of abandoning projects threatening your journey? Steady? Calm? What projects would you choose if you were free of those threats? On the next page, write a description of what your day would look like unhurried, with moments of connection to the environment around you, and instances of playfulness.

Navigating Time

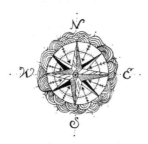

Who forces time is pushed back by time; who yields to time finds time on his side.
—The Talmud

Have you ever timed how long it takes you to do things? I do mean this literally. Have you considered using a measuring device—such as a mobile phone or a kitchen timer—and researching exactly how long an activity takes?

For example, how long does it take to wash, dry, fold, and put away laundry? Get gas? Drive to the grocery store and back again? Wake up, drink a cup of coffee, and check email or news? What about watering plants, picking a recipe for dinner, preparing breakfast on a Sunday, reading for what feels like a good long while, taking a strenuous walk, saying hello and catching up with a coworker or neighbor, or preparing your lunch for the next day?

If you've ever experienced "time fog," you know that state in which you're convinced you can clean the bathroom, vacuum, do two loads of laundry, and then run to the grocery store and back home (as well as unload the groceries) all in forty-five minutes. Time fog is a form of magical thinking. Once in a time fog, even if someone on the outside attempts to convince you otherwise by telling you that you don't have enough time, you'll reject their statement about "reality" and "time" for two reasons: one, it all *has* to get done, time be damned; and two, you actually believe you can *will* it to happen.

We want to fit it all in. We don't want to hear that it won't work.

There's no shame in that scenario; it is, honestly, wonderful that we want to do *so* much. The only wrinkle is time. Time is real; no amount of magical thinking will change it, and so the key is to understand time—and your interaction with it—more clearly.

FOUR DAYS IN YOUR LIFE

I now challenge you to record how you spend your time for four days. You'll do this in half-hour segments which will capture both the big and the small pictures of your life, yet not the minutia of, say, trips to the bathroom. If you're supposed to be working—that is, you're sitting at your desk but you're daydreaming, write down "work" but also make a note or symbol for "daydreaming" if that feels important to you.

You may choose any four days you wish, but I ask that you include a Sunday. Why? Because Sundays are notoriously shapeless, challenging days in civilized society, and that makes them ideal for self-study.

It's important to note that this exercise doesn't have predictable results, and it's also not a planning tool. So record what actually happens, not what *should* happen or what you hope will happen. This is likewise not a to-do list, but rather a record of how you spent this time.

Recording how you spend each half hour for four days may be surprisingly difficult because making a record like this means objectively observing yourself as well as facing facts, which is rather tough to do. If you forget or miss part of a day, simply start recording again as soon as you're aware of it.

A variety of feelings may arise as you do this; don't be too surprised by that. Be open to whatever comes up and regard your thoughts and feelings with curiosity and compassion. Patterns may come to light and you will be able to draw conclusions from the data you record about your days. Trust this process, and I promise it will be eye-opening for you.

....
day

GREETINGS, NEW DAY. IT'S TIME TO WAKE UP.

_____:00   ....

_____:30   ....

_____:00   ....

_____:30   ....

_____:00   ....

_____:30   ....

_____:00   ....

_____:30   ....

_____:00   ....

_____:30   ....

_____:00   ....

_____:30   ....

-- SIXTH HOUR --

_____:00   ....

_____:30   ....

_____:00   ....

_____:30   ....

_____:00   ....

_____:30   ....

_____:00   ....

_____:30   ....

_____:00   ....

_____:30   ....

_____:00   ....

_____:30   ....

-– 12TH HOUR –-

_____:00   ....

_____:30   ....

_____:00   ....

_____:30   ....

_____:00   ....

_____:30   ....

_____:00   ....

_____:30   ....

-– 16TH HOUR, TIME FOR EIGHT HOURS OF DEEP SLEEP. –-

....
day

GREETINGS, NEW DAY. IT'S TIME TO WAKE UP.

_____:00   ....

_____:30   ....

_____:00   ....

_____:30   ....

_____:00   ....

_____:30   ....

_____:00   ....

_____:30   ....

_____:00   ....

_____:30   ....

_____:00   ....

_____:30   ....

-– SIXTH HOUR –-

_____:00   ....

_____:30   ....

_____:00   ....

_____:30   ....

_____:00   ....

_____:30   ....

_____:00   ....

_____:30   ....

_____:00   ....

_____:30   ....

_____:00   ....

_____:30   ....

-— 12TH HOUR —-

_____:00 ....

_____:30 ....

_____:00 ....

_____:30 ....

_____:00 ....

_____:30 ....

_____:00 ....

_____:30 ....

-— 16TH HOUR, TIME FOR EIGHT HOURS OF DEEP SLEEP. —-

....
day

GREETINGS, NEW DAY. IT'S TIME TO WAKE UP.

_____:00   ....

_____:30   ....

_____:00   ....

_____:30   ....

_____:00   ....

_____:30   ....

_____:00   ....

_____:30   ....

_____:00   ....

_____:30   ....

_____:00   ....

_____:30   ....

-- SIXTH HOUR --

_____:00   ....

_____:30   ....

_____:00   ....

_____:30   ....

_____:00   ....

_____:30   ....

_____:00   ....

_____:30   ....

_____:00   ....

_____:30   ....

_____:00   ....

_____:30   ....

-− 12TH HOUR −-

_____:00   ....

_____:30   ....

_____:00   ....

_____:30   ....

_____:00   ....

_____:30   ....

_____:00   ....

_____:30   ....

-− 16TH HOUR, TIME FOR EIGHT HOURS OF DEEP SLEEP. −-

....
day

GREETINGS, NEW DAY. IT'S TIME TO WAKE UP.

_____:00   ....

_____:30   ....

_____:00   ....

_____:30   ....

_____:00   ....

_____:30   ....

_____:00   ....

_____:30   ....

_____:00   ....

_____:30   ....

_____:00   ....

_____:30   ....

-– SIXTH HOUR –-

_____:00   ....

_____:30   ....

_____:00   ....

_____:30   ....

_____:00   ....

_____:30   ....

_____:00   ....

_____:30   ....

_____:00   ....

_____:30   ....

_____:00   ....

_____:30   ....

-— 12TH HOUR —-

_____:00 ....

_____:30 ....

_____:00 ....

_____:30 ....

_____:00 ....

_____:30 ....

_____:00 ....

_____:30 ....

-— 16TH HOUR, TIME FOR EIGHT HOURS OF DEEP SLEEP. —-

YOU IN TIME

Consider these additional questions as you contemplate how you occupy time:

- How much time do you have for personal reflection?

- How much time do you spend connecting with others?

- In what instances do you try to cheat time or magically compress it?

- Where are there opportunities to free up bits of time?

- How do you approach large chunks of free, unstructured time?

- How comfortable are you being idle?

SPENDING TIME

Once you've studied four of your days, reflect on what you learned. What did you notice, feel, or want? What about the hours in a day—your use of them and your relationship to them—surprised, interested, or intrigued you?

There's room for squeezing, shifting, and sneaking in moments of great power into the course of a day—whether physical, creative, or spiritual. Such sneakiness will amplify your sense of being alive.

The hours in a day are not negotiable—everything takes time.

Hesitation to speak the word "no" disappears when, right there in black and white for all to see, you are clearly <u>too busy</u> for a "yes."

If you are exhausted and craving more time to yourself, there is a very real reason why. Discover that reason.

TIME LOG

Paying bills may have a "feels like" number of hours that in reality only takes thirty minutes. Shine light on such illusions by noting how long your tasks actually take.

TASK   TIME TAKEN   NOTES

....

                                                     ....

                                                     ....

                                                     ....

....

                                                     ....

                                                     ....

                                                     ....

....

                                                     ....

                                                     ....

                                                     ....

....

                                                     ....

                                                     ....

                                                     ....

TASK	TIME TAKEN	NOTES
....	....	....
		....
		....
		....
....	....	....
		....
		....
		....
....	....	....
		....
		....
		....
....	....	....
		....
		....
		....
....	....	....
		....
		....
		....

TIME WHEEL

Another way of looking at time is seeing it in wheel form. You can shade in or color in the areas of the wheel that represent sleep, work, or play for this 24-hour day and see where your hours are spent.

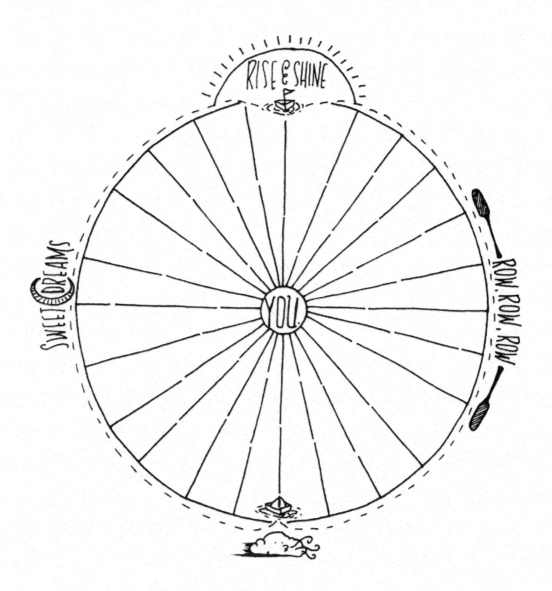

LIFE IS CONTINUOUS

Life can be represented and understood by a spiral, or gyre. This is not a way of suggesting that life is "spiraling" out of control; rather, it is a law of nature that things unfurl, go around and around, expand, and re-turn in cycles. You can find the spiral form repre-sented in the natural world —in seashells, ferns, pine-cones, pineapples, cauli-flower, mushrooms, and even within our inner ear, hurricanes, and galaxies in space.

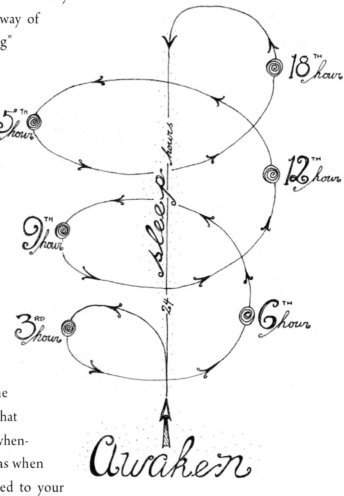

Consider a day in your life in spiral form. What if the "beginning" of your day were that moment when you awakened, when-ever that is, and the "ending" was when you went to sleep and returned to your unconscious? Though you might occupy many of the same places in a day, none of the hours are exactly the same, nor are your physical and emotional energies, which make subtle (or not so subtle) shifts throughout the day.

Spirals run their course and then they repeat, infinitely. Throughout the day—and throughout life—we often navigate the same territory, yet *we* are a bit different. The spiral represents that sameness/difference well.

Creativity sometimes needs the protection of darkness, of being ignored.

That is very obvious in the natural tendency many artists and writers have not to show their paintings or writings before they are finished.

Until then they cannot stand even positive reactions.

The passionate reactions of people to a painting, the exclamation,

"Oh, this is wonderful!" may, even if meant in a positive way,

entirely destroy the chiaroscuro, the mystical hidden weaving of fantasy which

the artist needs . . . Thus if you notice an unconscious fantasy coming up within

you, you would be wise not to interpret it at once.

Do not say that you know what it is and force it into consciousness.

Just let it live with you, leaving it in the half-dark,

carry it with you and watch where it is going or what it is driving at.

—MARIE-LOUISE VON FRANZ, "THE INTERPRETATION OF FAIRY TALES"

Wading into Uncharted Territory

No one looks like You, so look as much like yourself as possible.

Making mistakes is an art. No two mistakes are alike. Notice the uniqueness of your way.

Take responsibility for your actions; be the owner of your actions.

Everyone is wrong sometimes. Be the first to say you're wrong.

Speak your truth quietly and without apology.

Communicate plainly.

Eat a piece of ripe, organic fruit today. Steam and eat a vegetable. Eat a small salad.

Sip some water.

Listen keenly to another person, hear them, and ask for more. Wonder about others.

Cultivate your quiet side. Observe! Look around. Be a quiet observer.

In everything, slow down.

Create personal spaces that feel good to you. Create environments that speak of you.

Touch your skin—your toes, face, and even your hair. Rub your neck, shoulders, and
forearms. Give hugs. Hug yourself!

Say good-bye early, go home, and curl up with a book
(someone else can stay till the end of the party).

Take a sight or hearing break and connect deeply with your remaining senses
(in the kitchen or outdoors).

Offer your help to others and share your skills,
without expectation or a requirement of reciprocation.

Give yourself plenty of time to prepare.

Help yourself get places on time, or ... arrive early.

Spontaneity and control are two forces that will never join. Meet often with spontaneity.

Remind yourself to play, to be goofy, and to practice the art of silliness.

On Caring for Yourself

The answers you get depend on the questions you ask.
—Thomas Kuhn

When you begin the process of taking care of yourself, you may find there's a loneliness to it or feel that you are choosing yourself over others. Yet *you* and *others* aren't mutually exclusive. When you choose to listen to your inner self, seeking to know what you need and fortifying your intuition, you are choosing to center yourself, to become anchored and self-knowing, rather than do what you suspect, guess, or "know" others around you want. This work can feel like leaving the group, turning your back on a pact with a tribe. Yet you must save yourself whether or not departure becomes part of your journey.

If you grew up in an environment in which you were only accepted or praised for being or behaving a certain way, you might sense how significant and powerful the jump from *their needs* to *your intuition* is. It's huge, and the jump can save your life. It can afford you the ability to really breathe, and to feel less confined, fuzzy-headed, anxious, and oppressed by the expectations of others (real or imagined). The mindset required to survive a dysfunctional family got you through but left you unevolved, and that same mindset will undermine healthy communication and satisfaction in adulthood. Evolution and self-care are essential.

Sitting right next to that feeling of loss about not having "good parenting" you might find a feeling of possibility sitting there too. Why? Because you have a clean slate; you can do things how you like and apply what works for you because you're not utilizing the map your parents used. There is freedom in that, so go map-less and seek yourself.

It's your walkabout.

Why is it so difficult to care for ourselves? We might agree that eating well and getting exercise each day is important, and even vital to good health, and yet we struggle against it. Many of us fear that it's selfish, or that we'll be accused of selfishness if we care for ourselves. We sometimes love-hate ourselves because it *seems* "easier" to suffer, to stay un-changed, to wait, to daydream and to postpone, and yet, anything we do that takes effort and takes us out of our comfort zone will pay the greatest dividends. Avoiding change and day-dreaming instead is only a quick fix—or merely a quick distraction.

So what does behaving like you care about yourself look like? Sometimes it's going to the party, while other times it's leaving the party before the end. It's calling a friend without anything to report, simply to discover how they are, what's on their mind, what's new; it's picking up the phone when a friend calls you. At times it means saying, *Why not?* and other times, *No way.* There's no prescription for how to approach treating yourself well; certainly no one size fits all. For some of us more time alone—and to champion your need for that —is the key, while for others it may mean more time with friends or enjoyable family members in your circle.

No matter what it means for you, if you're willing to risk a little fear in caring for yourself, no subsequent risk will ever be as scary.

The foundations of self-esteem are acting as if you care for yourself and acting accord-ing to your own personal belief system—or your code. These actions, if I do most of them each day, keep me feeling right. Here are some acts of self-care:

- ⋆   Sleep eight hours.

- ⋆   Drink water.

- ⋆   Eat some broccoli and nuts, and drink some tea.

- ⋆   Find out how at least one friend is doing and listen to them.

- ⋆   Journal each morning.

- ⋆   Go for a hike, walk, or do 20 minutes of cardio.

- ⋆   Take a moment for gratitude.

- ⋆   Arrive early.

- ⋆   Experience an idea, read about ideas, or exchange ideas with someone.

IS IT SELFISH?

When you're working on your self-esteem from a few different angles—like straightening a bedspread by pulling the folds and wrinkles out from all sides of the bed until all lies flat— you're performing incremental work that strengthens and rises, plateau to plateau, over time. If you're ever challenged by another person for behaving "selfishly" during an act of self-care, beware; that person is unconsciously baiting you and making a play to unseat your self-esteem. Acts of self-care reflect healthy self-esteem. When others don't have that, they attack it.

If your friend or mate doesn't want to wait a half hour so that you can sunbathe before going to run errands together, you can decide to stay back and feel good about your decision. If you're teased about "acting like a diva," you can reply, "Indeed." If the comment feels like a jab, you can say, "It sounds like you're teasing me. Are you?" Usually, when someone accuses you of selfishness, they actually mean, "I wish I could give myself permission to do what you're doing," so another tack could be to speak to their unspoken wish. For example, you could say, "I give you permission to be horribly indulgent and lie here in the sun with me. The sun insists upon it." Or you could say, "Would you prefer to relax right now and run errands after?"

Free yourself of any question of whether you deserve to take care of yourself, or to take care of yourself in particular ways. Reject the notion that you don't have a right to the time needed for you, and lay aside any doubt that self-care is something non-negotiable.

Write down what you need in order to care for yourself. What do you need to hear? To say? To eat? To see? To do? Write down what actions do it for you, write down what helps you stay even-keeled. Even if your self-care includes solitary quiet time that you think your spouse or children won't appreciate, write it down.

take good care

Remember your Pledge of Self-Healing?
Turn back to page 23 and reread it now.

Fundamental Self-Esteem

Self-esteem is a manifestation of your spirit in action.
—Carolyn Myss

Do you know what self-esteem is or how it differs from self-confidence? The two terms are used interchangeably, yet they are in actuality completely different. Self-confidence is one-dimensional and simple, a display. Someone who speaks confidently, for example, displays certainty about what they're saying. In our culture we place high value on a person who exudes self-confidence, believing it indicates that he or she is someone we can trust—with our money, our safety, our communities—while we tend not to immediately trust the quiet, secure, respectful types who seem to lack it.

Because you can see self-confidence more readily than you can self-esteem, you won't know for sure that someone has self-esteem until you witness their actions. In the alcoholic or dysfunctional family system self-esteem is rare, so don't be shocked if you had no one to model *true* self-esteem for you, or if you mistakenly equated self-confident, authoritarian, and "suggestion-of-violence" parenting with strength.

Self-esteem cultivation requires much, much more than saying "no," and it goes beyond, and deeper than, setting up boundaries. You can say "no" and erect boundaries whether or not you actually have true, fundamental self-esteem, as it exists in the manifestations of your choices and behaviors. In short, our self-esteem is apparent and reflected by what we do. Handling yourself in conversations and in performing tasks—as well as within relationships and responsibilities—with care, honesty, and courage is evidence of self-esteem, not to mention that caring for yourself is as well.

Self-esteem operates on an internal mechanism for self-respect and action that is felt, not seen, much as a compass works. You could also think of self-esteem like a level, the bubble-and-line indicator that verifies whether a shelf is even or a picture on the wall is straight. As a compass deep in your center, self-esteem can guide you and inform your actions, and keep you oriented if you refer to it, acknowledge it, and honor it. Until our fundamental self-esteem is operational, we remain in conflict with taking care of ourselves in the areas of getting ample sleep, eating real food, and/or speaking truthfully.

Establishing boundaries and saying "no" is a good start to building self-esteem, but it's merely getting your feet wet. Once you've learned how to put those "defensive" aspects of it to use, it's time to wade out further and move into the "offensive" or proactive benefits of healthy self-esteem. This is when you are swimming in life, not avoiding it, because you have learned this: you've become buoyant enough in your self that there is no situation you cannot navigate by consulting and acting upon your self-esteem.

Your Compass, Your North

If you imagine a compass, and North is "you" and your *right* direction, then think about how your actions, reactions, and choices affect that arrow pointing north.

There are times when your actions are an act of saying "no" that are fueled by self-esteem. For example, you might decide to stop dating someone you've been seeing exclusively for a few months because lately it hasn't felt right; themes of anger, control, and negativity are seeping in, and you want to end the relationship. Or you might decide to stop cultivating a new friendship with someone who seemed like a potential friend, because lately themes of gossip, criticism, and drama have crept in, and you'd rather cultivate a new friendship with someone who uplifts you.

Self-esteem is what guides you through life to behave in ways that might be in conflict with what another person wants from you or what you feel the situation calls for. You act upon what seems to be true and right—what is in line with *your* truth—despite the fact that at times you will struggle within yourself. For example, a part of you may want something—say, a healthy relationship—while another part of you deeply craves immediate gratification—the compliments, the touch, the attention of another person.

Your compass, your self-esteem, lives in you and guides you, just as others are guided by their compass. When we don't respect what one another's self-esteem requires, conflict arises, which is typically a result of your self-esteem not being valued or regarded as valid by another person. This disregard can be inflicted *upon* you or *by* you, so it's important to be self-aware.

You Must Be the First to Respect Your Needs

Let's say you're at a community event with a group of friends, such as a county fair, parade, or tour. There usually comes a time when some people are hungry and others are not, or when part of the group wants to go one way and others want to go in the opposite direction. The person whose compass is informing them that they're hungry will get crabby and possibly resentful if they ignore their bodily need. Yet the not-hungry person may also get crabby or resentful if they go along and eat when they don't want to. Hunger is a simple example because it's a need that's more easily identifiable than, say, a need for time alone. If taking action to address your hunger gets intercepted by others' needs, you may indeed eventually get to feed yourself, but you might be so terribly hungry by then that it's not going to be without stress. You may be happy you've avoided selfishness, stuck with the group, and didn't ruffle anyone's feathers, but how do you feel? Were you operating with regard and value for yourself, or did you hang yourself out to dry? Were your needs and those of the group truly mutually exclusive?

What do a breakup and getting hungry have in common? Both involve parting ways with another person or group, only in one case it's permanently and in the other it's temporarily. Each also involves checking with one's self, asking questions such as, "How do I feel in light of the anger and controlling behavior I'm sensing?" or "How urgent is my hunger?" and then taking action on the result in keeping with your personal needs—your North.

Always abide the non-negotiable physical needs of hunger, going to the bathroom, and getting rest and sleep.

Ask yourself this: Do I believe that cultivating my interests has value? If you don't deeply value the importance of the pursuit of your interests, there's no use arguing about it with others; in any situation in which you're figuring out how to prioritize people, needs, and activities, you will quickly trade your priorities for everyone else's if you don't value your needs as equal to theirs.

Great anxiety comes up with regard to getting one's needs met if you grew up in a dysfunctional environment. In a chaotic home occupied by self-centered people, the alcoholic's (or narcissist's) need for reassurance and attention is so out of balance that the family sacrifices their own needs in order to keep the peace, to keep that person "happy." Over time, growing up in this kind of environment leads to difficulty with identifying our own needs, to mistrusting our instincts, and to not valuing our needs. It's no wonder we look (unconsciously) for relationships that have a thread of chaos running through them, for environments and communities in which we "bypass" our needs and focus on keeping the "whole" calm, or on soothing needy people. We may even be drawn to being around big problems—think of your personal equivalent of a restaurant kitchen or emergency room.

We are used to operating in modes in which our needs, both sensing and voicing them, are secondary, if even part of the conversation at all. We begin to believe *as long as everyone else is happy, that's all that matters,* and that fact becomes soothing in and of itself—that *everyone else* is satisfied, even though *your* needs aren't met. At times, wants can feel like, or appear to be, needs. This is because wants offer that soothing sensation, which is really just a temporary soothing. That is seductive indeed. If you're trying to resolve and grow out of a chaotic childhood because you desperately want soothing, you reach for things that comfort you (short-term gain) rather than build a strong foundation (long game). In short, quick-fix soothing is understandable, yet it is a fleeting, short-term fix and never more.

YOUR NEEDS

Nine times out of ten, someone who accuses you of selfishness is engaged in manipulative behavior, whether consciously or unconsciously, and may not value their own needs (because they didn't learn to), and that's why it's so important that you become solid, that you value your needs, that you respect your wants. Once we're solid, the attacks on "selfishness" cease.

If you live in the western hemisphere, you know wants—they're rampant in our society —while needs are simple and not particularly numerous.

WANT	NEED
iPhone	Connection with others
Dining out	Food
McMansion	Housing – a "roof"
BMW	Transportation
Yoga retreat	Physical activity/exercise

Conflict can occur when you (or someone else) chooses to regard a need as a want. For example, say you're on a road trip and your bladder is full. That's a need. If you believe it's a need, you can communicate it and regard it as one. "I need to stop for the bathroom."

A kind person is going to say, "Should I pull to the side of the road now, or can we go another ten minutes and find a restaurant?" Someone who is unclear on the value of needs might say, "If we stop we'll be late—can't you hold it?" When someone makes your need a problem or a headache, there's conflict. And this includes you: if your need is something you have shame about or are unwelcoming of, that's a conflict within. If you don't value your needs, it becomes confusing to others how to take action.

Your Code & Your Rights

Self-esteem is a manifestation of your code of conduct—or rather, your values and beliefs, which are fairly fixed, like North on a compass.

If you believe your needs are real and valid, that will guide your behavior. If you believe needs should come before wants (say packing your lunch rather than buying it), it will inform your course of action and guide you through the gray area. Say, for example, your coworkers are going out to lunch, but you don't want to spend the money because it will strain your budget. If you allow that to guide you, you'll decline the invitation in some form. That may mean that you'll walk over with the group and just order tea or something light, or that you'll simply say, "I can't join you but thanks for the invitation!"

If you compromise your code, your self-esteem takes a blow. That's not "bad," but it's stressful. It creates a strain on your spirit.

The reason self-esteem is "cultivated," that it is grown, nurtured, and made vigorous, is because each time you act on your self-esteem and let it inform your actions, you grow and strengthen its roots. Think of it as a practice that isn't always perfect but that becomes nearly indestructible once it becomes body memory—a natural act like riding a bike, having sex, or traveling and knowing how to find your way around new towns—it becomes a part of your fiber.

You have a right to:

* a healthy and pleasurable relationship
* feel good living inside your body
* express your needs
* be treated with respect
* good nutrition
* be listened to

* self-expression
* the pursuit of your interests, curiosities, and dreams
* safety
* time to relax
* pleasure

Now, write down your rights in your own words on the next page.

"I have a right to... "

LIFE, LIBERTY, AND THE PURSUIT OF HAPPINESS

As humans we have fundamental needs that are also considered rights, whether by the government, our culture, or families. Those rights include food, shelter, and clothing; a meaningful life; love and a sense of belonging to a group, a tribe, or a community; personal power and freedom; and the pursuit of a livelihood and making a contribution to your family, community, or humankind.

For each category on the next page, write about how you'd like to honor, cultivate, or tweak your pursuit of each of those rights.

food, shelter, & clothing:

creating meaning & spirit:

love & belonging:

power & freedom:

livelihood & contribution:

On Parenting Yourself

The great pleasure of a dog is that you may make a fool of yourself with him
and not only will he not scold you, but he will make a fool of himself, too.
—Samuel Butler

Believing that you can't do—or can't have—things because "they" said so is succumbing to an expired drama. A lot of us are going onstage in our daily lives and acting in a play that is no longer running. All of the characters, as well as the audience, are long gone (until, perhaps, you go stay with family). Why would you still recite old lines just because you memorized them?

The idea of being your own parent and growing yourself up is all about taking the reins. Embracing the work that wasn't done for you by your parents is a big step; it is indeed disappointing that they didn't get the job done, but somebody has got to finish it. That somebody is, of course, you. And, honestly, could you pick a better parent?

Parenting yourself is a healing adventure. It's a dialogue between you—as you are in the here and now, and your child self—the child you met in the first section of this book and carry around inside. This dialogue is important, powerful, and should be considered sacred. As you cultivate your ability to guide yourself, it becomes a bypass so that in time it's your voice and no one else's that reaches you, resounds in your mind, and guides you.

What does "self-parenting" mean? Rather than think of yourself as a drill sergeant, think of yourself as a cooking instructor, dog trainer, or yoga instructor. Treat yourself with respect and encouragement. There has been enough shame, bizarre discipline, and extreme emotion heaped onto your head, and now as your own guide, counsel, confidant, buddy, mentor, friend, coach, and/or lover, you can navigate life as a loved and curious person.

This isn't to say that you should avoid being firm with yourself, but it means letting go of harsh discipline; being firm with yourself can be gentle and loving. For example, if you get a feeling of calm pride when you get home and see a made bed and clean bathroom (as opposed to towels and clothes on the floor), then in the morning you'd say to yourself, "If you make the bed, even just straighten it up by fluffing the pillows and pulling the blankets flat, you'll feel good when you get home after a long day of work." Or, "You're totally tired and want nothing more than to curl up with a blanket and magazine right now, but if you push yourself to grocery shop tonight, you'll be stress-free about dinner for the next three nights. That's a bigger payoff."

If you help yourself prepare in advance and pave the way for a smooth night, for the next day, or even for the week, you're not only being a kind parent to yourself, but you're also reducing chaos and drama. Conversely, if you live one moment to the next all the time, you'll remain in the chaos of crisis-living. Moving out of reaction mode and into action mode is essential to healing, as well as a key ingredient of self-parenting.

BECOME YOUR OWN KIND, NURTURING PARENT

If it were up to you to parent yourself, be a friend to yourself, and encourage and look out for yourself from now and for the rest of your days, what would that look like?

Your definition of that will evolve over time, but the next page offers some starter ideas.

A kind, nurturing parent will:

*   agree that it's okay to leave a place when you've had enough

*   support you in trusting your gut about things

*   know there's no better teacher than mistakes and vulnerability

*   remind you that it's okay and normal to have feelings

*   remind you that you're not defined by your feelings, age, race, past, or class

*   sit with you quietly while you mourn, cry, or feel panicked

*   applaud you and celebrate you when you do big things!

*   remind you that "You can do this!" in all things that lead you to your bliss

As your own kind and nurturing parent, you can practice self-care in any of the following ways:

*   Get up in time to have a good morning and get to where you're going on time.

*   Feed yourself a nutritious breakfast free of anxiety-producing chemicals (e.g., sugar and carbs).

*   Take notes at a meeting, just in case! That's an act of looking out for yourself.

*   Think to yourself, "Getting up early can be tough, and I did it! Way to go!"

*   Go to bed on time so that you get the rest your body and mind need.

*   Grocery shop for the week on Sunday.

*   Think through the day ahead so that you're mentally prepared for it and unsurprised.

Luckily, there are always opportunities to take a compassionate approach to your self-parenting. When you've overindulged during the holidays or on a vacation, or gotten out of your workout routine or slipped up on saving money each month, you have opportunities to acknowledge the behavior compassionately rather than attack your whole self.

Perhaps say, "That was too much food and now you have a stomachache and can't zip your pants, but you're still sweet and humans do these things," rather than, "You're a glutton and a fatso."

Sometimes people overindulge while on vacation; you don't have to beat yourself up over it. While you're extending compassion to yourself, why not also ask yourself, "Might there be a reason why I overindulged? Is that something to ponder?" Self-parenting means taking care to check in with yourself, ask questions and be curious, but to refrain from accusing.

If friends invite you to an event and you don't want to go, you can consult your kind and compassionate inner parent, who might advise, "You will probably have a great time, but won't if you don't go," or might offer, "It's okay to skip this one and get a night of rest. You need it."

Here's an example of applying your own compassionate self-parenting solutions to the following scenarios:

Job Interview	"Prepare, trust your gut, and interview them."
New Love	"It's okay to be vulnerable. Get to know this person. Be sure you feel respected and actually like him/her. Take it slow."
Adventure	"Learn a lot! Prepare. Talk with others. Do your research."
Public Speaking	"They love you—just be totally yourself. And prepare."
Performance	"It'll be a rush! Prepare and you'll feel confident. Go, you!"
House Shopping	"You might need to look at 50 houses, and the right one will come at just the right moment. Do your research, but trust your gut too."

Now write down your own version of a loving parent's words:

Job Interview	Prepare, know your value/strength ask them ?'s too (need to know if you want to work there/fit in.
New Love	Take your time / get to know them their plans thoughts good • bad's) If you feel like you're trying to fix them or pity them run if they disi rest / not repeat run!
Adventure	It'll be scary but prepare for the things you can control — know that good things come after from discomfort / new things
Public Speaking	Prepare / know what your saying + why It is scary — pick a few faces in the crowd that seem to be listening. it that doesn't work — image all naked!
Performance	You've worked hard for this, have confidence in yourself! #1 is NOT the goal — being your best is . . .
House Shopping	

If it occurs to you that you can treat others well by applying some of these approaches, you are quite right. It will become natural and gratifying to pay the compassion and respect forward.

LOOKING OUT FOR YOURSELF

If you were to speak to yourself as a kind, compassionate, and encouraging parent, what might you say to yourself in the following scenarios?

You're at a party full of new people and you feel self-conscious and shy:

It's been a few months since you had that breakup and you're still not over it:

The alarm has gone off and you're not getting up:

A coworker asks you to lunch but you're engrossed in your work:

A bill arrives that you're not able to pay immediately:

There's an issue you'd like to discuss with your partner:

A good friend tells you she is moving away in a month:

Your employer praises your performance:

Thank him/her for noticing / ~~the~~ use words as
a continued motivator, /feel _validated_ by my work

Your birthday is coming up and you want it to be special:

Plan a party only the best people for you
don't do it all yourself!!!

You're starting to worry that your coworkers don't like you:

You're worried that you might be acting self-destructively:

You want to buy something big and need to save up for it:

You feel like reigniting your sex life:

You are feeling down and wondering if your fatigue and social withdrawal are signs of depression:

You're feeling that something is not quite right about your health:

You want to enjoy this moment and be present:

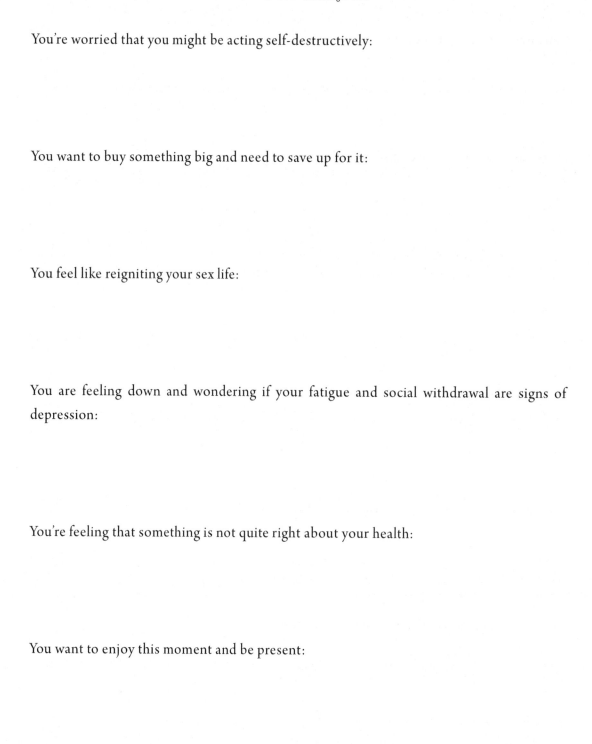

CARE AND FEEDING

Yes, you are what you eat. But just as integral is that you are what you love . . .
Love is the strongest driving force for the body's energetic balance, healing process,
disease prevention, cellular rejuvenation, organ vitality, blood cleansing,
molecular revitalization and vibrational freedom.
—DR. GILLIAN McKEITH

Many years ago, during my last visit with my mother, I saw her eat only two foods over the course of a three-day weekend: popcorn and Diet Coke slushies. Of course, slushies are made by freezing Coke in a 30-ounce plastic cup, which you then eat with a fork. She also chain-smoked. She was thin, always had been, and her face was made up like a clown (due to the poor lighting in her apartment and her glaucoma). She spent a day badgering me for a ride to her dealer so that she could buy marijuana. Her state was breathtakingly sad, and absurd too. By the end of the weekend I'd succeeded in convincing her that hydration was a thing. I believe she added water to her diet. There was that.

Your mind and body aren't separate entities; they are a system that works together. If you want to feel good, eat well—period. This is another case where we get a double whammy because our culture sends extremely mixed messages about food (be skinny/eat cheeseburgers) and dysfunctional families tend to fail hard at teaching children how to care and feed themselves because they are struggling with it themselves—if not flat out abusing food.

If you are someone who knows anxiety and the panic that runaway anxiety can lead to, you're in the right place—and you are in good company! I know anxiety; I have known panic attacks. I also know three substances that can bring about a panic-attack-like state in the body:

*   coffee
*   sugar
*   chocolate

Short list, right? (My mistress, chocolate, of course contains both sugar and caffeine, but deserves its own category because chocolate is *that* mysterious, special, and seductive.) A cup of coffee isn't going to send me into a panic—but three or more could, particularly if there's no food (protein) in my body.

I tend to value moderation, though I was not raised to; most children of alcoholics and otherwise rigid and conditional childhoods tend toward black-and-white thinking when something is out of balance in their life. For example, when an adult child begins a workout schedule, it's every day and intense. When someone crosses them, that person is "dead to me." When they make a mistake, they are a "terrible person." The terms moderation, ramping up gradually, compassionate, gentle, and measured are not part of their vocabulary.

While I sometimes get it wrong and overdo it or take a week off sugar completely before a presentation or race, I'd rather have coffee, chocolate, and sugar in moderation so that I can have a dialogue with myself about what feels like enough, what I'm really craving, or what stopping at or just before satisfaction feels like. If you want to and can eliminate coffee and sugar from your diet completely, that's fine; some might find zero-tolerance somewhat easier for starters because moderation is tricky living in an indulgent culture. Figure out what, for you, is the most compassionate approach to your consumption of substances like coffee and sugar and go from there. As you pinpoint your own limits, sensitivities, and reactions to those substances, it's important to know how they impact your physiology so that you can cure—and prevent—excessive, or unnecessary stress for yourself.

Before you say, "I must *quit* sugar!" consider an approach of moderation rather than an all-or-nothing course of action. For example, instead of *removing* chocolate, focus instead on *adding* something, and thereby nudging sugar into a smaller place in your diet. You might do this by adding lean protein, a new vegetable, or legumes (lentils) to your diet. Compare choosing what you put into your body to when people you're fond of start showing up at a gathering—how you forget how distracting that toxic cousin is once enjoyable people arrive. Give yourself options. Crowd out the bad.

IN PRAISE OF BROCCOLI

Before I learned how to prevent panic attacks, I would "come down" from the near-death paralysis of anxiety run wild into panic by a bowl of steamed broccoli. Broccoli became my anxiety antidote. I try to eat broccoli every other day, and I swear it keeps my moods, blood sugar, and energy levels even-keeled.

So maybe you fried your nerves and mind and energy this morning by guzzling coffee and had a chocolate chip scone. Compassion for your beautiful, important soul means you can realign and reset the sails at any time. The day isn't lost! Broccoli can be consumed and nourish the body and soul long before sundown comes.

If you're not yet tuned in to it, figure out your healing food. Mine is lightly steamed broccoli that's still a bit crunchy. I also find herbal tea to be relaxing as a transition between work and errands (chamomile, ginger, mint, licorice, and orange are favorites). Discover how you feel after trying out a variety of typically healing foods, such as:

* almonds

* pumpkin or sunflower seeds

* cabbage, fennel, peas, spinach, nettle

* miso or tomato soup

* herbal tea

* broccoli or sweet potatoes

* steel cut oatmeal

* chickpeas, black-eyed peas, lentils

* dried apricots, plums, oranges

I call them healing because they're nutrient rich, low on the glycemic index (won't trigger a blood sugar spike), and are simple, bare, one-ingredient foods. The difference between a "comfort food" and a "healing food" is that you won't feel full after consuming a healing food, nor are you drowning anything out. With a "comfort food" you're complementing the act of tuning out and curling up into a form of hibernation, whereas with a healing food, you're turning your physiology to an even tone, removing the static, clearing your head, and giving your spirit a loving lift.

Find out which foods work for you and which don't, and treat yourself right. It's simple, in the sense that we all know well that each day we benefit from consuming fresh (organic) vegetables and fruit, our bodies appreciate it. We know that by avoiding soda, as well as boxed, bagged, and otherwise packaged foods, and by cooking for ourselves, we are treating ourselves well.

On the following page, write down foods that you know make you feel good, cared for, and balanced.

We also benefit from moving our bodies—we know it makes us feel great. Walking is ideal, especially if that walk takes you uphill. So is swimming. Jogging and meditation are two additional ones, both of which are helpful if you have anxiety. Jogging can get you out of your head, and so can meditation. Both clear the mind of thoughts for a time.

So, do you really need to buy ten diet books when you already know the two core things you must do: eat fresh food and move your body? If you want a third, it's this: breathe. Armed with these three basic elements, you already have valuable knowledge about how to take care of yourself.

Breathing Exercise

Do this sitting up, or standing, with your eyes closed (open is fine if you're gazing loosely upon one point). You can also rest the tip of your tongue on the dip of your palate just behind your teeth, which opens air passages.

Let your mouth be softly closed and begin to inhale slowly through your nostrils by letting your body fill with the breath bottom to top—down in your belly first and then up into your lungs like a vessel fills with water, from the bottom up to the top.

Now exhale. Let the breath go, slowly, from your nose like a long ribbon in the breeze.

Breathe like this for seven breaths. Take these seven breaths once a day, or once an hour.

* If you're wound up, tense, or angry, then do this: purse your lips and push all the air out in a single forceful gust from your gut, completely emptying your lungs. *Pfffhoooof.*

CRAVINGS

I have never known anyone who cooks or makes love from a manual.
—ISABEL ALLENDE

"Treat me right." That's what my body sings to me. My mind craves information that surprises and delights me, that fills me with a sense of wonder. My muscles crave exercise, to be stretched, used, and to be oxygenated. My arms and body crave skin to sleep against and caress. My lungs crave expansion and contraction. My fingers crave pens, pencils, and keys. My eyes crave color. What do you crave? What do your brain, muscles, body, and spirit each long for?

Make a record of what you crave. Does your nose desire the aroma of cinnamon or to inhale dry warm air? Does your chest crave an embrace? Your arms, do they ache for a bear hug or to hang long and stretch? Regard each zone of your body and the senses that enhance it, imagining what each one craves. If your muscles could talk, what would they ask for? What about your brain? Does it crave learning a language or to freely wonder? Your feet? Would they ask for sand to curl and squeeze their toes around?

Hear your cravings.

There's no rush to complete each of these in one sitting. Take a walk and ponder the answers to one or two; contemplate them while meditating, cooking, or gardening. The answers will come to you with clarity if not urgency when they come, and they will vary over time. Write about your specific cravings on the next page.

When a Toe Craves the Sand

- scalp...
- Eyes...
- NOSE...
- mouth...
- 👄...
- TONGUE...
- HEAD...
- EARS...
- arms...
- CHEST...
- BACK...
- 🖐️...
- fingers...
- MUSCLES...
- BUTT...
- genitals...
- LEGS...
- THIGHS...
- feet...
- toes...

The Doldrums

Jung has said that to be in a situation where there is no way out, or to be in a conflict where there is no solution, is the classical beginning of the process of individuation. It is meant to be a situation without solution: the unconscious wants the hopeless conflict in order to put ego-consciousness up against the wall ...

—Dr. Marie-Louise von Franz

Treating yourself well isn't merely a matter of knowing what's best and then following it. There are times we act out or rebel; we disappoint ourselves when we expect to do right or to be perfect constantly and continuously. The reason why we rebel against our good intentions is never obvious—it could be our shadow side taking its turn. In his book, *Owning Your Own Shadow*, Robert Johnson writes that our shadow is:

> the dumping ground for all those characteristics of our personality that we disown . . . these disowned parts are extremely valuable and cannot be disregarded . . . To honor and accept one's own shadow is a profound spiritual discipline. It is whole-making and thus holy and the most important experience of a lifetime.

It's important to see your spirit's rebellion as an opportunity for understanding. When it occurs, acknowledge it as real and investigate further—with curiosity. When you do, toward transformation your path will lead.

When we experience a period of not treating ourselves well, whether staying up too late, not eating well, or by physical inaction, our mood, energy, and spirit sink.

If you were to inquire within and get a sense of what is going on, you might ask yourself:

What am I feeling?

Where am I feeling it?

What am I really craving?

What do I wish were happening right now?

What do I miss?

What do I want?

What does my deepest self want?

As you answer these questions, talk to yourself in a wise, nurturing, and guiding voice. Here's an example:

YOU:

So it looks like you're eating ice cream. Cherry Garcia, huh? It's the middle of the day, isn't it? And if I'm right, it's your third pint of Ben & Jerry's this week. It's hard to ignore how much fat and sugar is going into your body. You had planned to watch Netflix without ice cream but couldn't resist it. That's happening a lot this week. What's going on? What are you craving? Sometimes you overindulge on sugar when you're not getting time to nurture yourself, like to take a bath or draw; or when you're feeling cheated out of something in life, or resentful, or really behind at work; or even tired and working on too little sleep. What are you craving? What do you really want? Because you took the day off to work on your personal project, and you're acting like it's a different kind of vacation day ... the nap, sweets, and lying in the sun where you can't realistically work comfortably for very long.

YOU IN RESPONSE:

I'm feeling heavy, like a great weight is attached to my ankles. And so fatigued. I'm worried it's depression showing up. I'm expecting myself to pivot from work to this project and to the other project and to just go, shift, pivot, go, go, go and I need a break. I have so much to do! Yet I am craving a vacation. I want a beach to walk along with no deadlines waiting. I'm craving swimming in a hotel pool and to be a kid again, to not come when called and to keep swimming and pretending I don't have to get out. One last handstand. One last somersault.

If I were a child again (for once!) I could be carefree. No burdens!

You know, this dialogue is kind of a break. It's got me thinking: I should go for a thirty-minute walk and get some perspective right now. I'll feel less powerless then, and I'll get some oxygen—away from the computer screen.

UPON RETURN:

I feel better. Nothing has changed, but I feel refreshed. I feel listened to, acknowledged, and capable again.

You can do your own contemplation when the time is right on this page and the next.

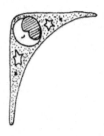

The Intrigue of "No"

Life is full of pauses.
Breaks are a normal, natural phenomenon, and they are just what you need when you are being pressured for an opinion or a decision.
—Patrick Fanning

Uh-uh. Pardon me? Nah. Say that again? Nope. Can't. I'm all set. Actually I'm busy. Let's talk later. I'm not up for that. Yeah, no. Take me off your list. No receipt. Wish I could. Next time. If only. That's not going to happen. Heck no. No way, man. Totally not. Like, never. When hell freezes over. In a word? *No.*

Saying no is hard at times. The key is to practice saying "no" in non-threatening, simple everyday situations, and to back it up, if not express most of it, with your body language. Once you have some practice with it, saying "no" during important moments in your life and communications will go a lot easier and be a more rewarding situation. But a word of advice if this isn't your strong suit: take all the time you need to practice with the small stuff before tackling harder, more volatile situations.

Opportunities for practicing your "no's" abound. Here are just a few:

Grocery store (samples)	Body shop
Downtown	Café
Gym	Retail store (membership card)
Newspaper kiosk	Restaurant
Bank teller	Teenage children
Hair salon	Coworkers
Food truck	Neighbor
Deli counter	Door-to-door solicitor

As you play with saying "no," you'll begin to experience that it's okay to say it, and when you get good results, you'll realize that "no" isn't the end of the world; rather, it's communication that's actually a positive. Why? You're expressing yourself, for one. Two, you're being honest.

When you say "no" or "no, thanks," you are in reality expressing a preference—that is, what you *do* like. If you say "no" to cream and sugar, you're actually saying, "I like black coffee." Saying "no" can express "I prefer to have my hair off my ears," or "I'm happiest relaxing with a book right now."

If it helps to ease what can sometimes feel like life and death when saying "no," swap "no" for a voiced preference like the above, saying, "Actually, I'd like . . ."

Saying "no" helps others take action, or not take action, as the case may be; the word "no" helps others learn about you, sweet you. Have you ever noticed that when others use the word "no" you actually feel a wave of respect for them, that you notice their self-respect?

AH, NO...

For the next five days, say "no" in as many forms and as often as you can. Write down the circumstance and make a few notes about how it felt.

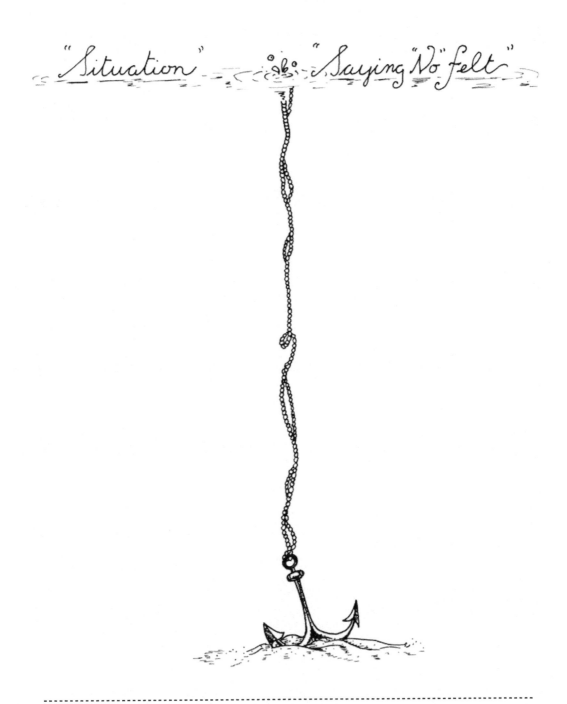

"*Situation*" & "*Saying "No" felt*"

One secret about the word no is that it sometimes makes you intriguing to others.

Unconditional Love for Yourself

The work of love involves giving yourself time. How much time do you spend with yourself?
Do you take time for proper rest and relaxation or do you drive yourself unmercifully?
—John Bradshaw

You can learn to love yourself and feel kindly toward yourself, even during such moments as spilling your first coffee of the day, snapping at a stranger on the sidewalk, or extending your middle finger at a driver on the road. When you can love yourself, you begin to see that you are made of many parts—some crabby, some kind—and you learn to view yourself with compassion. At some point the thought will occur to you, "Maybe that driver is having a bad morning and is beloved to the people in his life," and that's when the beauty really begins to burst and lift up not only you, but those you are striving to love, raise, and get to know.

Do you love yourself unconditionally? Or do you reject yourself entirely when you do something like eat high-fat or super-sugary foods? Do you consider yourself a failure if you have a slow, distracted week at work? If so, you're probably loving yourself based on conditions and from a perfectionist's mind frame. This is not a surprise for anyone who grew up within a household of conditional love. People who have never been exposed to the effects of growing up in a rigid, dysfunctional home are sometimes shocked by the capacity for self-loathing that those who grew up with it are capable of.

If your parents lived by the conditional love and affection code, you're likely still living by it yourself. Conditional means *on a condition*, such as, "I'll give you affection if you compliment me, and I'll withhold it if you don't." Or, "I'll tell you I'm proud of you if you bring home a great report card." Or, "I'll tell you I love you if you act how I need you to act." And on, and on.

If you expect to get certain reactions and praise from your mate based on "good" behavior, you were probably raised in an environment where conditional love and affection were in play. If you think, "I didn't work out today. I'm a shit," it's the same story, where conditional, all-or-nothing, black-and-white rules abounded. If you've ever turned that ugliness on others (indeed, the ones you love) and attacked or judged someone's whole being based on a mistake, comment, or action, you could be acting from a conditional code. This all hinges on placing perfection on a pedestal.

The great news, however, is that it's your life and your story now, so you can make a new code. You can learn to love yourself. Your only job is to begin.

COMPASSIONATE THINKING

One of the hallmarks of a compassionate approach to regarding yourself and thinking about your life and actions is that it's *of the moment*. A compassionate thought will be very specific and lacking in judgment and emotional backstory, sounding something like:

I'll think it over.

I haven't made up my mind yet.

I'll let you know.

Maybe!

You know, if I picked up all the books and magazines and straightened the pillows on the couch, my house would easily look neat and tidy.

Sometimes my audiences don't get my jokes, and sometimes they do—either way, I'm glad about my work.

There are times when my friends can't get together with me, but I value our relationships.

I missed the first two classes of chess, but I'm not going to quit the class—I'll jump in, get help, and find my way.

I value, love, and respect myself no matter what.

My love is not dependent on "good" behavior, money-making, or achievement, but on my simply being me, and alive.

I love myself when I'm making ends meet, or not.

I love myself most compassionately during my rough times.

RIGID THINKING

Rigid thinking can also be called all-or-nothing or black-and-white thinking. It often involves "ifs" and "thens" (conditions), such as:

If I'm late for the interview, why go at all?

I slipped up on my diet. I guess that's over.

Joe can't make the party. It'll suck without him.

She's late? She's no good.

You're with us or against us.

Your house is always a mess.

I'm a terrible cook.

If I can't keep my cool, I'll turn crazy.

If I don't look conventionally attractive for my mate, I'll end up alone.

If I don't act strong and solve problems for my mate, I won't be desired.

If my mate doesn't offer to help with the dishes, no sex tonight.

My appearance must be just right.

My actions must be just right.

If I give in to my kids' wants, they won't abandon me when they leave home.

If my partner catches me relaxing, I'll seem lazy.

I can't ask a friend for help because I haven't given them anything.

If these people don't like me, I'm unlikeable.

If people saw my house, they wouldn't want to know me.

ONWARDS TOWARD COMPASSION!

It takes practice to stop the habit of thinking the conditional thoughts that keep you bound to the mast. The way to unwind is by forming a new habit.

Recollect a few recent conditional thoughts you've speared yourself or another person with, and rework them into compassionate, flexible, generous views. Consider conditional thinking that you engage in around the following categories:

- ✳ Job and achievements

- ✳ Love and affection

- ✳ Personal and spiritual

- ✳ Body and mind/Physical and mental

- ✳ Finances and money

Here are two examples of conditional thoughts transformed into compassionate self-parenting:

CONDITIONAL THOUGHT

If I nap during the day, I'm a Lazy Person.

COMPASSIONATE THOUGHT

I am a person who sometimes naps, and I love that about myself. Napping doesn't make me lazy; it makes me a well-rested person who has a better chance of thinking clearly and staying balanced. So, not only is it "normal" to nap, it's a unique part of what makes me "me" and offers me an opportunity to nurture myself too.

- - - - - - - - - - - - - -

CONDITIONAL THOUGHT

I planned to work on my book today but did other stuff, knowing better. Seems I'm still defeatist and sabotaging myself. I don't see how I'll ever complete a project. I'm no writer.

COMPASSIONATE THOUGHT

I made a plan and didn't stick to it. It happens. Since it's bothering me a bit, I'm going to check in with myself and see if anything else is going on, if there are feelings I need to tend to—was I distracted, scared, or feeling rebellious? I'll then find a way to do some of what I'd planned to, and then schedule the rest for another time in the next three days. Distraction happens. I'm not a robot, after all; I'm human. There's no "writer" mold that exists and no rulebook for how to behave.

CONDITIONAL THOUGHT

COMPASSIONATE THOUGHT

- - - - - - - - - - - - - -

CONDITIONAL THOUGHT

COMPASSIONATE THOUGHT

- - - - - - - - - - - - - -

CONDITIONAL THOUGHT

COMPASSIONATE THOUGHT

TAKING RESPONSIBILITY

*The willingness to accept responsibility for one's own life
is the source from which self-respect springs.*

—JOAN DIDION

Taking responsibility for yourself, your actions, and life is a hallmark of adulthood. This can be challenging as there's not much emphasis placed on dependability, credibility, or regard for responsibility in a chaotic or dysfunctional family system.

The definition of responsibility includes the words accountability, bond, duty, concern, obligation, part, role, bit, task, bailiwick, jurisdiction, onus, trust, and beat. You might notice that "perfect" is not one of the words on the list.

A lot of us associate responsibility with blame and are familiar with phrases like, "You need to take responsibility for your actions!" without a grasp of what it means. We grew up thinking that taking responsibility means admitting we've broken the neighbor's window and facing our punishment. Sure, that's part of the definition, but there's also the other side of the coin—the positive, self-respect-generating aspects of responsibility. Taking responsibility isn't taking on blame, but rather removing blame from the equation.

In most chaotic or conditional-love-based families, the concept of responsibility is twisted. Often, responsibility masquerades as a distraction—or scapegoating—in which one person becomes the symbol of a "problem" whether or not they want to or have anything to do with the problem. I had a few experiences of admitting to a false wrongdoing while I was growing up because I was expected to; the consequence for denying responsibility was too frightening. So how was I to learn that responsibility was positive or that it could free and empower me when the truth of the situation was irrelevant? The silent message was "you'll take responsibility when someone needs you to, so you won't be in charge of that." It's likely that I thought when people acknowledged responsibility for things, they were lying! Bottom line: if you grow up in an environment that's shame based and everyone is on pins and needles, then responsibility is not only a low priority, but it's also unhelpful in a survival environment.

Acts of responsibility include:

* Being specific
* Keeping in touch
* Communicating ("I'm running late.")
* Asking questions
* Offering to help
* Showing up when you say you will

* Picking up after yourself
* Returning a phone call
* Expressing your desires
* Wearing a condom
* Explaining why you disagree
* Saying hello
* Saying goodbye

When you grow up with rage or unpredictability even for the smallest things, such as "Who the hell left the light on!?" it's scary to contemplate showing your whole hand. When you grow up being yelled at or physically abandoned or threatened for saying what your truth is, it takes a lot of courage to begin taking responsibility for what you've done and what you think because you've been chastised for what others *said* you were doing or thinking. It's therefore easy to fear you'll be yelled at just like you were in the past. So, clearly, vulnerability comes with this responsibility-taking territory. Try to remember that you can be and feel both responsible and vulnerable at the same time; when you do, you'll soon feel courageous and buoyed by how others react—admiration, laughter, truth-telling, their best selves, relief, and love all come into play.

Once you're solid with it for yourself, you can claim responsibility to your family/clan, coworkers, your community, the environment, and more.

In the space below, write about ways in which you want to become responsible to yourself.

Embracing Your Flaws

Like the erratic movements of the rotating arm of the dishwasher, miscalculations can make the machine more efficient. The same could be said of the unpredictable swirl of leaves in autumn, the random elegance of clouds, or the imperfect symmetry of a beautiful face.
Never underestimate what looks like a fumble.
—Véronique Vienne, The Art of Imperfection

A pit bull was up for adoption a couple of years ago. I watched a video of her playing with her foster owners quite a few times, and I was drawn to her because she was unique—having one blue eye and one brown eye—and because she was clearly gentle and playful. Her flaws drew me in.

Likewise, my cat, Wanda Honeybelly, has a white (though she is brown), pinch-sized tuft of fur on her back that stands up on end. Once, after I'd first adopted her, I trimmed the tuft to minimize it, to "normalize" her coat of fur. Silly me. The trim didn't erase the flaw; it merely became a shorter tuft of fur. I now value it because it is uniquely *hers*, just as I cherish the crooked front tooth of a man I adore. Flaws aren't problems; in fact, they can be triggers for adoration, features that endear us to one another. Flaws remind us of our appreciation for another human being (or pet) and for ourselves.

The following excerpt is from the book *The Art of Imperfection: Simple Ways to Make Peace with Yourself,* by Véronique Vienne.

In Islamic art, small flaws abound in what look like the most luxurious carpets, pottery, and mosaics. Artists are urged to make mistakes on purpose, to remind observers that God alone is perfection.

In music, notes that deviate from an established pattern are often used to create emotional tension. Beethoven was fond of this technique. In the Third Symphony's "Funeral March," for example, he replaced sounds with silences to express the mounting sense of sorrow in that piece.

In literature, James Joyce was the champion of the intentional error. For him, mistakes were "portals of discovery." In Ulysses in particular, typos, misspellings, and absence of punctuation add to the insightfulness of his prose.

Let me share a few of my flaws with you. These flaws of mine are unique features of who I am and my philosophy has come to be: "I love me, so of course I love my flaws." Do they mean that I have no strengths? Hardly. All it means is that I'm not perfect.

You know *you're* not perfect, right?

And you know you're not supposed to be perfect, right?

I interrupt people.

I smile a lot, and even more so when I'm nervous.

My face is asymmetrical.

I overdo it on thank you gifts and probably alienate people in doing so.

I have a gummy smile.

I speak my mind.

My opinion often shows on my face.

I'm critical and analytical.

I can't remember people's names.

I get lost in my imagination.

I need to be quiet in the morning.

I have a stretched out mommy belly.

I crack jokes.

I'm kinda short.

Flaws are not terrible things. They are traits that show you aren't exactly like the next person. I'm sure there are a lot of aspects about me and my personality that annoy people; some I can control and some I can't.

But flaws illustrate uniqueness, not negatives or things to hide or try to fix. Flaws are attributes that when someone loves you truly, they know it's you and they accept it all—as you learn to do for yourself.

We perceive flaws subjectively because they are dictated by the culture in which we live. Yet who's to say what's "beautiful?" The Academy? The critics? Our families? Your neighbor? Wrong, wrong, and wrong. *You* decide that you're beautiful.

Try looking at your body naked without "cutting out" parts and simply see yourself. Artist Chuck Close said, "I have no intention of flattering people. I like wrinkles and crows' feet and flaws, and somebody should know, if I'm going to photograph them, that's what's going to show up."

If you've ever replied to a compliment by saying, "How can you think my body is beautiful?!" You can now shift your reaction to something more like, "I'm so glad you feel that way."

Fall in love. Be as foolish and joyful as a dog. Actor Ashton Kutcher says:

Vulnerability is the essence of romance. It's the art of being uncalculated, the willingness to look foolish, the courage to say, "This is me, and I'm interested in you enough to show you my flaws with the hope that you may embrace me for all that I am, but more important, all that I am not."

What might one say about her flaws? Here's an example:

> I have a matchless birthmark you cannot miss on my behind, a gummy smile that my grandmother called "homely" but is fabulous and puts others at ease, and a special extra pouch of skin under my left eye when I smile that's adorably asymmetrical. When I get excited I tend to interrupt people just to prove I'm perfectly imperfectly me.

Label and then pair your flaws with a fantastic adjective (ideas below), such as thrill-seeker's crows feet, bewitching post-baby belly, adorable lip curl, sexy crossed-eye, pride-inducing bosom, welcoming guffaw, etc.

ADJECTIVES	FLAWS
sexy	scar
humanizing	crooked tooth
cute	cowlick
distinguishing	missing finger
disarming	lazy eye
exceptional	bow legs
matchless	ample buttocks
rare	bunion
unprecedented	bosom
definitive	wrinkles
adorable	gray hair
hallmark	dark circles

On the next page, celebrate your unique traits in writing.

☆ My ^endearing personality ~~flaws~~ quirks:

☆ My physical ~~flaws~~ hallmarks:

Marilyn Monroe said, "I'm selfish, impatient, and a little insecure. I make mistakes, I am out of control and at times hard to handle. But if you can't handle me at my worst, then you sure as hell don't deserve me at my best."

A SPIRITUAL PRACTICE

My personal opinion is that the neutral position on the mood spectrum—what I call emotional
sea level—is not happiness but rather contentment and the calm acceptance that is the goal
of many kinds of spiritual practice.
—Dr. Andrew Weil

A spiritual practice is an action you take every day, one specifically aimed at
cultivating your connection to something beyond yourself, something greater than
you and the whole of humankind. It can take many forms and shapes, depending on what
moves your mind, heart, and soul and what it is that facilitates your connection to your
humanhood.

One person's spiritual practice may be a conversation with God while another person's
may be the cultivation of her inner goddess or god. And the concept of "god," too, can take
many forms: Great Spirit, Mother Earth, a saint, a deity, Iron John, Greater Society, or the
Unknown. Find your own way to behold how small and yet significant, how humble and
yet counted, you are. That's the key.

If you've heard of the book *Zen and the Art of Motorcycle Maintenance*, you know that a spiritual practice is not limited to activities like prayer or meditation. If you are present in the moment, you are practicing; you are stepping off the conveyor belt of your daily routine and walking through your front door, coming "home," reuniting with your Self, your spirit, your soul.

You can craft a spiritual practice from any of these acts:

GARDENING. Watering plants can be done in such a way that you're connecting your spirit to the greater Earth and to people who have come before and planted the soil, simply by watering and nothing more. Wendell Berry said, "We learn from our gardens to deal with the most urgent question of the time: How much is enough?"

MUSIC-MAKING. Hit a key on a piano. Strum a string on a ukelele. Drumming with your hands, especially, can be cathartic. Aldous Huxley said, "After silence, that which comes closest to expressing the inexpressible is music."

DANCE. Using movement, you can interpret a dream, act out the day's scenes, conversations, and feelings, or simply prance about the house in your underwear … or even less!

WALKING. The tempo of walking matches thinking nicely, yet there is life around you to notice, your own breath to appreciate as you place each foot upon the ground, and the Universe that encompasses the solid, ever-moving ground beneath you.

INTERACTION. You enjoy self-compassion when you give the benefit of the doubt to someone in the course of your daily interactions and when you observe what other humans are up to. On interacting with others, Eckhart Tolle writes:

When you give your fullest attention to whoever you are interacting with, you take past and future out of the relationship, except for practical matters. When you are fully present with everyone you meet, you relinquish the conceptual identity you made for them — your interpretation of who they are and what they did in the past — and are able to interact without the egoic movements of desire and fear. Attention, which is alert stillness, is the key.

MEDITATION. With meditation, you learn to quiet your mind and oh how the mind likes such a state. Every meditation is different, so if you're new to it, consider buying the small, simple beginner's book, *How to Meditate*, by Lawrence LeShan.

JOURNALING. Begin writing *I don't know what to write here!* and you will be surprised what comes next. Write "morning pages" or do free-writing in which you note your random thoughts without judgment. For ideas, refer to Natalie Goldberg's book *Writing Down the Bones* or *The Artist's Way* by Julia Cameron.

What does it feel like to be alive in this universe in which you exist?

PERFORMING A SPIRITUAL PRACTICE

Pick a spiritual practice and give it a try for a week. Write down what you think of it, then choose another to try out for a week. Repeat this for four weeks, each with a different practice, and record what it was like for you. Remember that a spiritual practice is just that —practicing doing it—as opposed to achieving it, perfecting it, or finishing it.

WEEK ONE SPIRITUAL PRACTICE ....

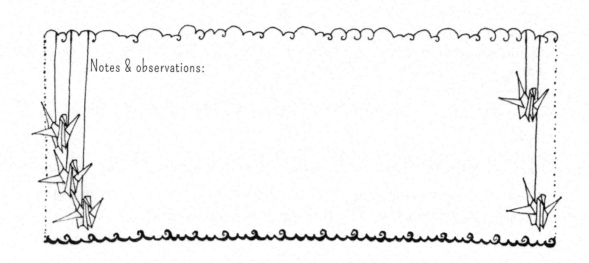

Notes & observations:

WEEK TWO SPIRITUAL PRACTICE ....

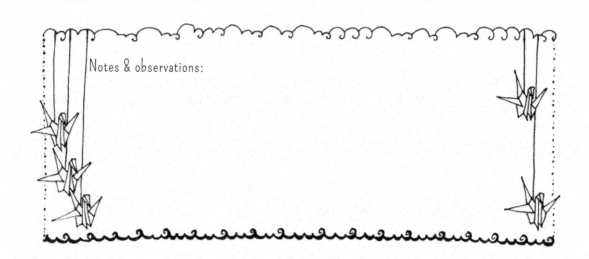

Notes & observations:

WEEK THREE SPIRITUAL PRACTICE --

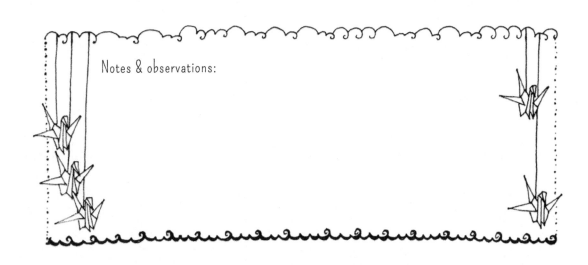

Notes & observations:

WEEK FOUR SPIRITUAL PRACTICE --

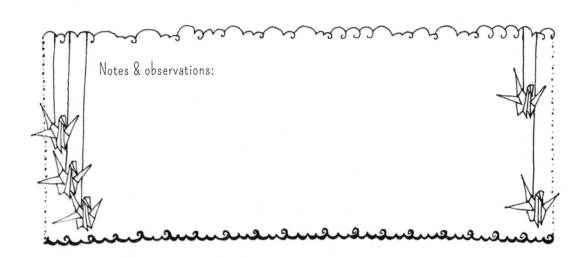

Notes & observations:

Gratitude

There is no special time or place for great realization. It's nothing more than parking your car, putting on your clothes, taking a walk.

—Charlotte Joko Beck

A *gratitude practice* is the act of being grateful. To be grateful is to consciously understand and acknowledge the significance of someone or something in your life, in the life of someone you care about, or in the world. The act of gratitude is to regard for a moment the components of life, your life, and choose to credit them, count them, and appreciate them. That's *gratitude.* The *practicing* of it is the act of taking a few moments every day, stepping off the path of your day's routine and quietly feeling huge appreciation for life and the things that comprise it. To practice something means to make a daily effort to do it.

That's all.

And it's big-huge!

Some people find it useful to hold something—such as a stone or a coin—in their hand when practicing gratitude, or to write as a way to focus their attention on the act of being grateful. (I say "act" because it may feel forced, at first, but that's okay.) Like a new pair of pants, trying novel ideas can feel stiff at first; it takes a few wearings to feel at ease in them.

Because our minds sometimes play habitual phrases and scenes that are often unhelpful and produce a chemical anxiety response in our bodies, practicing being grateful teaches our brains to change tracks, or to choose the track. But first we need to guide it. Eventually it will find the good groove naturally.

All you need is practice.

While gratitude may be reminiscent of the annually recited Thanksgiving dinner script, "I'm thankful for ... my family, my health, and the unconditional love of my dog," it is a useful template for beginning the practice of expressing gratitude.

What are you grateful for? That will vary. Depending on the day, I may have a feeling of deep gratitude for:

public art; street musicians; foods like the bread the bakers at Wildflower Bakery craft; the fact that people do try to find jobs they like and do projects they like, and that people do seek their bliss; quiet abandoned beaches; my able limbs; my hands; my health; that my art is portable; my son's humor; my son's life; his artistry; my son's laughter; the smile I shared with a stranger yesterday morning; my willing-ness to be alone and the courage that engenders; increasingly enjoyable moments with family and our recalibrated relationships; the conversation I had with a dear friend on Friday night; my faith in the Universe and its Way, especially when my faith in myself is weak and displaced; getting to witness the joy of two dogs playing on the beach last weekend; time with a group of friends who are accepting and loving and who genuinely enjoy each other's company; watching kids play by the water and create with sand, stones, and their imaginations, and the realization observing them brings: that we all get to be truly carefree in our lives, and that as children we don't care if what we create lasts beyond the afternoon!

Write about what gratitude is for you on the next page.

"I FEEL GRATITUDE FOR..."

CRAFTING A NURTURING ENVIRONMENT

I like an empty wall because I can imagine what I like on it.
—Georgia O'Keeffe

Do you live within a nurturing environment? Would you like to? Ask yourself these questions: what brings you comfort? A solid lock on the door? Flowerpots on the doorstep? A purring cat or woofing dog to greet you? What aromas put you at ease? In your living space, where are your beloved reading or music-listening spots—an old leather chair or a pile of pillows that you sink into? What colors, shapes, and objects do you see first when you arrive home? What defines "home" for you? What is your favorite, or coziest, space at home? Do you have one?

Some of us grew up with stand-at-attention types of "rigid" childhoods and tend not to relax easily. As a result, it might not have occurred to us to build nurturing spaces into our environments. But guess what? You can now. The first step is to remind yourself what you like and to learn what home means to you.

What colors draw you in? What textures delight your fingers? What sounds and objects make you smile? Spend time thinking about what makes a space feel "right" to you by studying other people's living spaces, magazines, catalogs, or decor websites. Sense what your favorite colors, textures, sounds, scents, and tastes are, and I mean *yours*, not what's trending. Pay attention to the smallest details you notice.

For example:

Colors	Textures	Sounds	Scents	Objects	Tastes
burnt orange	velvet	rain	lilac	books	dates
celery green	wool	typewriter	jasmine	fountain pen	olives

Make a record of the things that delight you:

Colors	Textures	Sounds	Scents	Objects	Tastes

"Home"

Now define, for yourself, what home means to you. Write down your unique and personal definition of home, including how you feel there and what differentiates it from every other place:

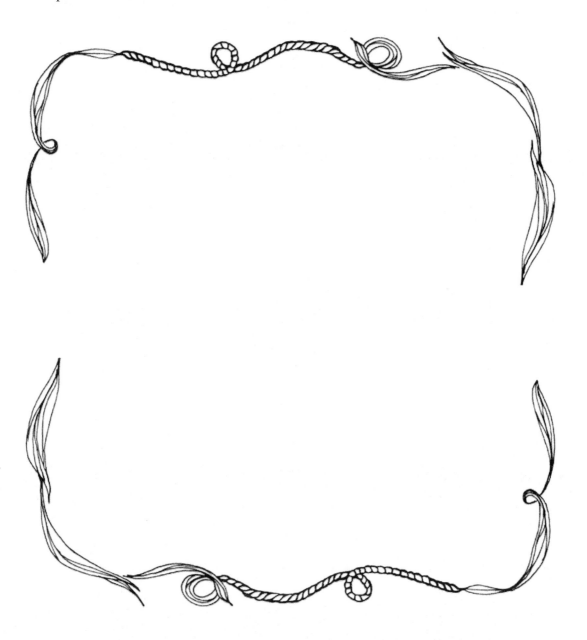

Bravely Sharing Your True Self with Others

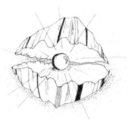

I love you.

—ANONYMOUS

As products of dysfunctional families, we have a tendency to not readily share ourselves. It's uncomfortable, scary, and can make us feel incredibly vulnerable. I know; I've been there. But now that you've been courageous enough to work through the exercises in this book—hopefully with some exciting, insightful breakthroughs—you can now begin to share thoughts and aspects of yourself with others by letting go bit by bit and becoming willing to be uncomfortable at times sharing something you fear isn't "normal." Why? Because I hope by now you realize that there is no normal. Everybody has "stuff" that sets them apart; their "stuff" might be different from yours, but we all have it just the same.

You expect others to show themselves to you, don't you? You want to know what you're getting, see who it is you're dealing with, talking to, falling in love with, caring for, etc. For those same reasons, you must show yourself as you are.

How can someone fall in love with you, which involves getting to know you, if you don't share yourself? Of course, perhaps one or two will walk away, but oh! Those who stay will have seen You. If you withhold, you remain "safe" but alone (and the "safe" part of that bargain is, of course, debatable).

Sharing yourself has the power to move mountains for your personal growth and healing. Standing up and saying "This is me" will be an act of love that allows others to see you—and thereby heal you. Your truth is home.

Now it's time to express who you really are, to share yourself, bit by bit, moment by moment, breath by breath. Look back through these pages; you'll find that much of the answer is already there.

I AM...

Our ability to find something to love, and to love again for the first time,
depends greatly on how we resolve and integrate where we've been before.
A great model for us exists in the chambered nautilus, an exquisite shell creature
that lives along the ocean floor. The nautilus is a deep-sea form of life that
inches like a soft man in a hard shell finding his prayers along the bottom.
Over time it builds a spiral shell, but always lives in the newest chamber.

The other chambers, they say, contain a gas or liquid that helps the nautilus
control its buoyancy. Even here, a mute lesson in how to use the past:
live in the most recent chamber and use the others to stay afloat.
Can we, in this way, build strong chambers for our traumas: not living there,
but breaking our past down till it is fluid enough to lose most of its weight?

Can we internalize where we've been enough to know that we are no longer
living there? When we can, life seems lighter. . . . only time can put the past in
perspective, and only when the past is behind us, and not before us, can we be
open enough and empty enough to truly feel what is about to happen.
Only by living in the freshest chamber of the heart can we love again and again
for the first time.

—MARK NEPO, THE BOOK OF AWAKENING

Self-Healing Vocabulary

Abandonment

Abandonment occurs when a parent or caretaker leaves a child or the person being cared for physically or in spirit. It can occur through leaving without notice, being present but emotionally vacant, or being present but intoxicated or high. Parents or partners who regularly use mood and physiology-altering substances to cope with their emotions spiritually abandon their children as well as their partners. To feel abandoned is to feel left behind and insignificant, untethered, and cut off.

Abusive Dynamic

A dynamic in which you and/or someone else acts from a spirit of manipulation, fear, and control, which can involve: taunting, shame, bullying, belittling, acting like a child as a parent, or using minimizing, insults, rumors, lies, or heightened, extreme emotions. Whether conscious or unconscious, the aim of abuse is to have power, control, or influence over the other person. It is an unhealthy dynamic that can be tempered with compassion, vulnerability, and honesty if the participants in the dynamic are ready to transform. An abusive dynamic can involve verbal insults or physical aggression, as well as suggestions and threats of violence, passive-aggressiveness, or the threat of abandonment.

Accountability

The act of owning one's own truth and of embracing responsibility and ownership of your actions, needs, and wants. It means being good to your word, doing what you say you will do—or plainly, honestly communicating why you cannot—and being willing to see how your words or actions have impacted another person. Being accountable is not accepting blame; it is a shame-free, honest act that removes blame from the equation.

ADDICTION

Being unable or unwilling to refrain from a substance or act and regularly seeking relief and escape from reality, feelings, or events through a substance or act. An addiction quietly takes priority over human interactions, intimacy, and responsibility by appearing to "heighten" a moment as it becomes irresistible and essential in ways one can inevitably find rationalizations for. Addictions eventually—and inevitably—become more powerful than their host. Some examples of addictive substances or acts are sex, sugar, daredevil excitement, shopping, debt, food, gambling, violence, gossip, alcohol, and drugs.

ANXIETY

A state of distracting, ongoing fear usually brought on by what-if-scenario thinking that the brain believes to be nearly real, and therefore causes the stress chemical cortisol to be released in the body. It is an emotional-physiological reaction of the body and mind to irrational thoughts, worries, substances, and outside stimuli that produces a fright, fight, or freeze response and can escalate into a panic attack. In short, it is emotional overwhelm.

BALANCE

The necessity and fact of balance can be seen in nature by way of the seasons, day and night, and the phases of the moon. A life of balance is manifested by taking time to be quiet following activity, eating simply after indulging, resting following work, listening as much as talking, and moving one's limbs after they have been sedentary. Balance includes enjoying creative and sensual aspects of one's humanhood as much as the analytical and intellectual spheres.

BENEFIT OF THE DOUBT

When you give someone the benefit of the doubt, or it's given to you, assumptions and conclusions are absent, as well as the emotions and reaction that accompany or are the result of making assumptions. When the benefit of the doubt is given, trust and compassion are activated, defensiveness is avoided, and true listening (also known as *love*) takes place.

CODEPENDENCY

A state in which you believe others cause your feelings, pain, or actions, or that you have the ability to control or influence the actions and feelings of others through obsession, powerful thinking, or control. We overcome codependency by taking ownership of our feelings and actions, by seeing and valuing our separateness from others, by accepting that others are their own entities, and by pursuing our bliss while encouraging others to pursue theirs. If you've ever heard, "So-and-so will be upset if you don't do such-and-such," you've been invited into codependent thinking.

COMPASSION

Living and acting from the belief that we all share common origins and a need for love, nourishment, and shelter. Living with compassion means embodying the understanding that not one of us is alone and that every one of us counts and is valid, deserving of kindness and understanding. Compassionate actions are kind, loving, obligation-free, and unconditional.

COMMITMENT

Choosing to give yourself to something in a wholehearted yet open-eyed, open-handed, and humble yet ambitious way over a period of time.

CONTENTMENT

Between the poles of upset and glee are the calm waters of contentment, in which one feels truly fine, even-keeled, satisfied, and in the simplest, most essential way *alive*.

DENIAL

To be in denial is to activate wishful thinking, pretending, and self-delusion when life presents challenges beyond one's comfort zone and ability to cope, or when one's beliefs and desires are challenged by events that they wish weren't occurring.

DEPRESSION

A state of being in which a person can't experience highs and lows of emotions, but rather lives in a muted emotional state. When depressed, a sense of helplessness and hopelessness permeates everything, as if nothing matters and never will; it's a state that endures for weeks, months, and sometimes years if not dealt with. Whereas Major Depression is a more devastating depression that impacts day-to-day functioning, Dysthymia is a milder "walking depression" that can last for long stretches of time and make one's daily life muted yet still livable.

DETACHMENT

When you detach from a person, a person's addiction, or a group, accepting that they exist as they are, doing what they will do—and you exist, but separately from them. You then can refocus on your own journey, actions, and health while allowing others to do the same. Detachment means accepting what is, allowing others their life choices as well as the consequences of those choices, and seizing your journey. The beauty of detachment is that it doesn't require forgiveness in order to take place, yet it frees you. The opposite of detachment? Obsession.

DISASSOCIATION

The state of going numb, the sensation of leaving one's body, or the shutdown of a part of your emotional self to cope with a situation. It can feel like entering a state of unreality or of having a fuzzy brain, and it can be triggered by highly stressful or abusive scenarios in which "going numb" enables survival of the moment or situation. (*See also* Post-Traumatic Stress Disorder).

DOMESTIC VIOLENCE

Physical violence—hitting or pushing—is an obvious form of domestic violence and abuse, but the definition of home-based violence is not limited to physical acts. Domestic violence includes many forms of control, intimidation, and manipulation, such as the threat of violence, aggression, hard pinching, threats, name-calling, isolation, stalking, taking money, bullying, bribes, taunting, and intimidation.

DYSFUNCTIONAL FAMILY

A family is dysfunctional if they lie, deny, blame, shame, or avoid certain topics to protect a secret or member of the family, prevent anger, or maintain homeostasis. People feel like they are "walking on eggshells" in dysfunctional families, feel generalized fear, and aren't accepted for who they really are, particularly when it doesn't support the family lie. There is typically a cycle of chaos in operation in dysfunctional families in which the members are always entering a state of chaos (or "excitement") or recovering from it. A dysfunctional family system includes a "perpetrator" or source, a "victim" or medium, and a supporting cast of perfectionists and scapegoats.

EMPATHY

A state of vulnerable and humble sharing of another person's state of being without judgment or caretaking, advice-giving, or minimizing. Empathy is judgment-free, fixing-free, and a quiet state of being *with* another person as they feel what they feel. We empathize when we enter the state or perspective of another person and connect with their experience.

FORGIVENESS

The act of choosing to release a resentment, fear, or troubling energy you've held tight and associated with a person or occurrence. When we forgive, we alter our relationship to our pain; we let go of the effect a situation had on us and recalibrate our perspective. To forgive is not to absolve another person for their actions, and forgiveness can occur independent of whether or not a person or entity related to your hurt has acknowledged their actions.

Gratitude

Reflecting on and acknowledging goodness in one's life and in living life. The mind frame of appreciation, awe, and love.

Grief

A state of mourning the absence of a person, animal, or experience—such as a certain kind of childhood—in which a deep sense of loss and profound separateness from the Other is felt. It differs from depression in its specificity to the loss of the Other and also in its phases, some of which take longer than others: denial and isolation; anger; bargaining; depression (worry, longing, and emptiness); and acceptance. Often the term "waves" is used to describe the behavior of grief in how it comes and goes and washes over a person.

Honesty

Living in honesty extends far beyond *not lying* as it involves forthrightness, being responsible, proactive, respectful, and kind with regard to your feelings, needs, and wants. Being honest includes expressing how you actually feel, without blame or requirements, as well as living in vulnerability, trusting in life, and extending the benefit of the doubt. Living in honesty is a means of trusting yourself and the Universe as an expression of self-care and love, one that fortifies self-esteem.

Humility

The embodiment of knowing you are equal to all others and living life in learner or "student" mode, embracing that you have much to learn no matter your current wisdom, and knowing that lessons may come from any source or person, without regard to their place or position in society. Humility is living from a place of self-esteem and calm while also being curious and teachable.

INNER CHILD

Your original and truest self, the Self you were born as, the Self beneath the armor, manipulation, anxiety, masks, and coping shell. Your inner child is the key to finding your way in life by uncloaking and befriending that curious, playful, and energetic being eagerly awaiting your permission to thrive.

INQUIRY

The process by which we ask ourselves questions in order to understand our motivations, feelings, and true desires. When feeling intense emotion or, in contrast, *no* emotion or emotional "numbness," inquiry can be the road to release, understanding, and transformation. Questions to ask during an inquiry process can include: What happened just before I got upset? How does my body feel right now? What would I say if I had a powerful voice right now? Am I overwhelmed? What do I want? What do I secretly desire? What does my Inner Child have to say about this? What assumptions are supporting how I think about this? Why am I upset?

INTIMACY

There are a great number of types of intimacy: emotional, intellectual, physical, personal, and of course, sexual. The common thread is closeness, presence, quiet vulnerability, being honest, and sharing one's Self—all in an unhurried, calm, and focused way.

"I" STATEMENTS

Sometimes called I-Messages, "I" statements are a communication tool that allows us to be heard and hear others without being distracted by blame. "I" statements assist us in being able to hear how another person feels, why, and what they need by reducing the distractions of defensiveness, blame, and victimhood. For example, "Why can't you be on time for me!?" conveys anger and blame but not much actionable information. However, reworded into an "I" statement, the message can be productive and convey feelings, needs, and wants. "I feel like a low priority when you're late to my house. Can I ask you to make

an effort to be on time?" "I" statements have a general blueprint of, "I feel ....
when .... and I'd prefer that ...."

KINDNESS

The embodiment of having genuine concern about someone, whether yourself or another person or animal. It is humbly showing concern without expectation of the kindness being reciprocated, and doing it for the sake of the kindness itself.

MANIPULATION

Attempting to influence or control the actions, decisions, thoughts, or feelings of another person through the use of criticism, compliments, bribes, praise, or with emotional or physical displays. Alternatively, it is being affected by the disingenuous actions of another person. Often terms like "or else" and "if" are used or are implied in an attempt at manipulation. When someone is struggling with self-acceptance or personal power, they'll use manipulation to fake those things and to feel in control.

MINDFULNESS

The art and practice of noticing that you are alive, paying attention to this very moment of aliveness without judging it or making meaning of it.

NARCISSIST

A narcissist sees their own self reflected when looking at others, rather than actually seeing the other. Narcissists crave acknowledgment and approval from others in order to maintain a sense of self, special-ness, and superiority. They are unable to cultivate deep, long-term intimate relationships and tend to be superficial and limited, serving the narcissist's needs; this is underscored by the narcissist's inability to relate to the feelings of others, have empathy, or foster understanding of the validity of other perspectives.

Needs

The things necessary not only for your ability to survive—such as physical safety—but in order to thrive in life. Physiological needs include air, water, food, clothing, and shelter; safety needs include job security, savings, and healthcare; needs for love and belonging include a connection to people, friends, community, and intimacy; the need for esteem includes respect, self-esteem, and a sense of competence and achievement; and the need for self-actualization includes deriving meaning from life and contributing to the greater good. (*See also* "Fundamental Self-Esteem," page 157.)

Panic Attack

In reaction to anxious thoughts, a state of physiological distress that sets in and seems to paralyze a person internally. This panic state can involve a racing heart; a sense of barely surviving; enduring a blotted-out, fuzzy, or spacey mind; or living in the past and future simultaneously, as if being pulled into a "what-if" black hole. During a panic attack, some people fear they are having, or are on the verge of having, a stroke or heart attack.

Physical Abuse

When you or someone else acts with physical aggression upon someone and imposes their will upon another person (child, adult, or elderly). Physical abuse typically occurs in a cycle: the peaceful honeymoon period > tension and buildup > chaos and incident > regret and apology > amnesia or forgetting > and then moves into the honeymoon period once again. Physical abuse includes slapping, punching, hair pulling, hard pinching, neck grabbing, throwing objects, preventing sleep, kicking, excessive cold or heat exposure, withholding food or medication, or exposure to excessive loud noises or music. (*See also* Domestic Violence.)

Post-Traumatic Stress Disorder (PTSD)

The state of having been psychologically altered and haunted by a disturbing experience. Some people with PTSD experience panic or physiological distress when recalling a traumatic event or re-experiencing a similar event, which may be characterized by nightmares and insomnia or by living "cocked," ready for a fight or conflict in a heightened fight, flight, or freeze response. Treatment for PTSD exists and includes choosing a therapist you thoroughly trust, telling your story so that it can be witnessed and discovering a way to make meaning of it, and reintegrating new life skills and practicing them over time.

Recovery

Actively healing wounds. When someone says they're in recovery, it often means they've made a commitment to a 12-step group process, whether Codependents Anonymous (CoDA), Adult Children of Alcoholics (ACA), or a similar group. It more broadly refers to a commitment to forging new emotional and physical pathways and habits in order to promote healing and enjoy an addiction-free life.

Resilience

An ability to navigate, deal with, and bounce back from change and adversity. Resilience can be learned; it can also be practiced by placing focus on identifying possibilities and positive, alternative outcomes when faced with adversity.

Responsible

Being true to one's word, committing to doing what you say you'll do for yourself and others, and owning your own actions with honesty, even when others cannot. It characterizes a person with an ability to think for one's self and choose a course of action consistent with agreements made with others or one's self, regardless of what others' choices are, as well as a person who operates with an inner mechanism of honor, purpose, or greater good.

SELF-DENIAL

A state of mind or action that involves convincing yourself that everything is fine, minimizing evidence and signs of problems, or being in a state of unwillingness to look at your life closely, openly, or from all angles. It involves avoiding outside opinion that might alter your "self-protective" thinking, which could include your own behavior, choices, or agreements, personal contracts, potential addiction to a substance, activity, or another person.

SELF-ESTEEM

Self-esteem is a direct pathway between your values, beliefs, and personal code and is manifested by your actions. It is the compass that guides your life choices and decisions and that fortifies your spirit.

SELF-MEDICATING

Ingesting sugar or other substances to alter your body's chemistry specifically as a means of alleviating stress, anxiety, depression, or of otherwise regulating your mood, which usually overlaps with addiction to the chief substance used.

SELF-PARENTING

Being engaged in an ongoing dialogue with yourself and your inner child about what you need and how you feel, and practicing acceptance of those things while encouraging yourself with kindness to take care of your physical, emotional, intellectual, spiritual, and sensual needs as you participate in life. It involves being a champion of yourself and taking care of yourself independent of how you were raised, bringing together self-esteem, self-care, and independence.

SELF-SABOTAGE

A belief that we have an inner desire to fail. When we stop moving forward because we don't know the next step in a project or don't truly want to be where we are, we call it "self-sabotage."

Sensuality

The slow savoring and enjoyment of experiences involving touch, sight, smell, sound, and taste as a celebration of being alive.

Shame

A deep, burning feeling of distress about one's actions and self-worth. Healthy shame is a form of humility, vulnerability, and honesty—such as realizing you weren't the top choice or rear-ending someone on the road—as reminders of your fallibility as a human (we still love ourselves and know our worth). But unhealthy shame hits with a toxicity that delivers a deep sense of unworthiness, as if we ourselves are a mistake, which can alienate us from our true self.

Sobriety

Being aware, tuned in, present, and free of alteration from substances. For alcoholics, sobriety means a lack of intoxication, or being alcohol-free. More generally, sobriety means being substance-free from alcohol, pain medication, sugar, marijuana, etc. When people talk about emotional sobriety, they're talking about living drama- and chaos-free, living a life in which feelings are felt, not avoided, and in which one is aware, present, responsible, and denial-free.

Spiritual Practice

An action taken to connect to one's humanity and the Universe as a part of a greater whole. This can be a daily meditation or it can be achieved through daily acts such as gardening, taking a walk, or swimming. A "practice" is doing something regularly and with commitment, but not with the goal of being perfect at it or reaching an endpoint.

SURVIVAL MODE

Living in reaction to things—such as to the past or to what others do, say, or expect—rather than taking independent action. Survival mode is living tied to the past, to what has just occurred, and to frustration with what one cannot control. When living life in survival mode, everyday tasks and responsibilities are fraught with difficulty, one's life becomes insular, and one finds him/herself navigating one interpersonal or work drama after another, as if a victim of those situations, rather than as a participant on some level.

THRIVING

One is thriving when he or she is grateful for opportunity, love, and life and is choosing to feel good things are possible. It is feeling pride in actively taking care of one's self and in choosing healing and responsibility for one's self. In avoiding situations and people that would chip away at your self-esteem, and living with humor, being in the here and now, and experiencing vulnerability as openness not as prey, you act from a place of compassion for yourself and for those you deem safe.

TRAUMA

A single or recurring upsetting event that so damages the body, mind, and spirit that, if left unresolved, can deeply influence one's life and ability to thrive. Trauma can persist in a painful and haunting way, often unseen to the outside world despite one's efforts to deny, ignore, or "pretend it away" over a lifetime. (*See also* PTSD.)

TRUTH

Your personal truth is your way of living in the world and doing what's right for you; it's your calling, your path. Your truth is an undeniable knowing, sense, or inkling—an often small, quiet, and patient inner sense. It is what's true for you no matter what others might wish, want, or attempt to recommend for you; it is a part of who you are and what you're capable of—a guiding feeling or understanding for living in a way that complements and enables you to identify, find, and act on your bliss. Your truth is what you believe, feel, and know without dispute.

Values

Your values are the deeply important, fixed beliefs that guide your life and actions. What you value may be a natural outgrowth or something you adopted from family or others, such as creativity, personal growth, friendships, excitement, financial success or security, privacy, pleasure, good food, knowledge, sobriety, competition, physical fitness, democracy, safety, etc. What you value can be discovered by examining your choices and action. If you value knowledge, but not competition as much, you'll spend your time at a party getting to know others' ideas as opposed to finding out how your achievements stack up against theirs. Similarly, if you value helping others but wealth not nearly as much, you may work teaching or rescuing animals; while you may wish you had more money, you nonetheless feel quite satisfied. Some of our values are complementary to those of people we love; when they're not, it may be an opportunity for compassion.

Verbal Abuse

Verbal abuse is communication empty of respect, compassion, and humility, reflecting an inability to regulate one's emotions, fear, or insecurity. One form of verbal abuse is passive-aggression and sarcasm; another is the "silent" treatment or stonewalling. Other forms of verbal abuse include conditional bargaining, such as "If you love me," or the minimization of another person or their feelings, such as "Don't be an idiot" or "You're making such a big deal out of this." Belittling and shaming would be, "You're no smarter than me," while blaming and blasting would sound like, "Why must you push my buttons?!" (*See also* "I" Statements.)

Victimhood

Victimhood is viewing one's self at the center of mishap and circumstances and as the one most harmed by circumstances, as if things happen "to" you rather than independently of you. A person is in victimhood when he or she identifies the source of hardships, problems, or pain as other people, groups, or inanimate objects, such as by saying, "This car has it out for me," "She doesn't want me to succeed," or "I bet this company would be happy to see me go." In victim mode, one forgets their personal power and ability to act on their own behalf, losing sight of their self-worth and accountability for their influence on their own life and the lives of others.

WANTS

After needs are met, wants are the icing on the cake—the activities, experiences, or engagements that you'd like to have for reasons that add to your sense of thriving as You. Wants characterize being alive, furthering your personal truth, and maximizing your bliss. You might need job security but *want* to help animals for a living or own your own business; you might need a place to live, but *want* to live closer to the center of town to be part of things. Wants reflect an intersection of your personal values, bliss, and self-esteem.

RECOMMENDED READING

Bassett, Lucinda. *From Panic to Power: Proven Techniques to Calm Your Anxieties, Conquer Your Fears, and Put You in Control of Your Life.* New York: HarperCollins, 2001.

Beattie, Melody. *Codependent No More: How to Stop Controlling Others and Start Caring for Yourself.* Center City: Hazelden, 1986.

Clarke, Jean Illsley and Dawson, Connie. *Growing Up Again: Parenting Ourselves, Parenting Our Children.* Center City: Hazelden, 1998.

Dayton, Tian. *The ACOA Trauma Syndrome: The Impact of Childhood Pain on Adult Relationships.* Deerfield Beach: HCI, 2012.

Dayton, Tian. *Emotional Sobriety: From Relationship Trauma to Resilience and Balance.* Deerfield Beach: HCI, 2007.

Fanning, Patrick and McKay, Matthew. *Self-Esteem: A Proven Program of Cognitive Techniques for Assessing, Improving and Maintaining Your Self-Esteem.* Oakland: New Harbinger Publications, 2000.

Fanning, Patrick and Frankfort, Lisa. *How to Stop Backing Down and Start Talking Back.* Oakland: New Harbinger Publications, 2005.

Johnson, Robert A. *Owning Your Own Shadow: Understanding the Dark Side of the Psyche.* San Francisco: HarperSanFrancisco, 2009.

Klipin, Judy. *Life Lessons for the Adult Child: Transforming a Challenging Childhood.* Johannesburg: Penguin, 2010.

Kritsberg, Wayne. *The Adult Children of Alcoholics Syndrome: A Step-by-Step Guide to Discovery and Recovery*. New York: Bantam, 1988.

Myss, Caroline. *Sacred Contracts: Awakening Your Divine Potential*. New York: Three Rivers Press, 2003.

Roth, Geneen. *When Food Is Love: Exploring the Relationship Between Eating and Intimacy*. New York: Plume, 1992.

Ruiz, Don Miguel and Mills, Janet. *The Mastery of Love: A Practical Guide to the Art of Relationship*. San Rafael: Amber-Allen, 1999.

Vavrichek, Sherrie M. *The Guide to Compassionate Assertiveness: How to Express Your Needs and Deal with Conflict While Keeping a Kind Heart*. Oakland: New Harbinger, 2012.

Whitfield, Charles L. *Healing the Child Within: Discovery and Recovery for Adult Children of Dysfunctional Families*. Deerfield Beach: HCI, 2006.

Woititz, Janet G. *Adult Children of Alcoholics*. Deerfield Beach: HCI, 1983.

Woititz, Janet G. *Lifeskills for Adult Children*. Deerfield Beach: HCI, 1990.

Woititz, Janet G. *The Intimacy Struggle: Revised and Expanded for All Adults*. Deerfield Beach: HCI, 1993.

About the Author

AMY EDEN is a writer, speaker, and workshop facilitator based in Petaluma, CA. She began her career in publishing in 1994, working for magazines, some of the earliest websites, and academic and professional publishers. Her nonfiction articles have been published in city and national magazines, and she holds a BA in English and an MFA in creative writing. You can find Amy's Ignite talk "Hacking the Phrase 'They Did the Best They Could'" and her self-help writing on the blog, www.guesswhatnormalis.com.

CPSIA information can be obtained
at www.ICGtesting.com
Printed in the USA
LVOW04s2356080217
523695LV00019B/569/P